Quietly At Work

TOWNSHIP GOVERNMENT
IN AMERICA

Quietly At Work

TOWNSHIP GOVERNMENT IN AMERICA

Monica Dwyer Abress

specialtypress

PUBLISHERS AND WHOLESALERS

Illustrations by John Valo

Special thanks to the Minnesota Historical Society for the use of photos.

Library of Congress Cataloging-in-Publication Data

Abress, Monica Dwyer, 1961-
    Quietly at Work: township government in America/by Monica Dwyer Abress
        p. cm.
    Includes index.
    ISBN 1-58007-032-9 (softcover)
    1. Local government--United States, I. Title.

JS418 .D96 2000
320.8'3'0973--dc21

99-086138

Published by:
        Specialty Press, Inc.
        11605 Kost Dam Road
        North Branch, MN 55056
        Phone 800-895-4585
        Fax 651-583-2023

Book Trade Distribution by:
        Voyageur Press
        123 North Second Street
        Stillwater, MN 55082
        Phone 800-888-9653
        Fax 651-430-2211

About the Author

 Monica Dwyer Abress was first elected township supervisor for Lent Township, Chisago County, Minnesota, in 1990 in a write-in campaign. Currently she is the chairperson of her township, a position she has held since 1997. Monica was recently elected to the board of directors for the Minnesota Association of Townships, representing the ten-county area of District 7. She also served as the secretary/treasurer for the Chisago County Association of Townships for three years. The managing editor for a small publisher, Monica resides in Minnesota with her husband and four beautiful daughters. Aside from township government, her daughters are her favorite subject.

Dedication

To Amanda, Aileen, Ann Marie, and Amy:

This book proves dreams do come true,
some just take longer than we want.

To Tim:

Thank you for standing by me as I
pursue my dreams.

Acknowledgments

Special recognition must be made to

Bill Bliss, chairman, Wabedo Township, Cass County, Minnesota
for countless hours of research and overall cheerleading,

and to

**Hamilton Brown, director of training and technical assistance,
National Association of Towns and Townships, Washington, DC**
for his enthusiastic support of this project from day one.

For help with research I want to thank:

Dan Beardsley, executive director,
Rhode Island League of Cities and Towns

Chas Bettendorf, teacher, North Branch High School,
North Branch, Minnesota

Dan Birdsall, land developer,
Forest Lake, Minnesota

Carol Bliss-Miller, teacher, Bagley High School,
Bagley, Minnesota

Thomas Bodden, manager of information and research,
Association of Towns of the State of New York

Thomas Bredeweg, executive director,
Iowa League of Cities

Gail Brock, executive director,
South Dakota Association of Towns and Townships

Ken Carty, communications associate,
Massachusetts Municipal Association

Michael Cerra, senior research associate,
New Jersey State League of Municipalities

Bridget Chard, chairperson, Sylvan Township,
Cass County, Minnesota

Paul Coates, director, Office of State and Local Government Programs,
Department of Political Science, Iowa State University

Michael Cochran, executive director,
Ohio Township Association

Deanna Cope, membership services administrator,
Indiana Township Association

John Dooley, attorney,
Minnesota Association of Townships

Daniel Emmons, president, Town of Elnora,
Daviess County, Indiana

Linda Fantin, reporter,
Salt Lake City Tribune, Utah

Jim Fisher, supervisor, McDavitt Township,
St. Louis County, Minnesota

David Fricke, executive director,
Minnesota Association of Townships

Kim Gulley, director of policy development and communications,
Kansas League of Municipalities

Bryan Hoime, clerk/treasurer, Overland Township,
Ramsey County, North Dakota

Sandra Hooker, chairperson, Medo Township,
Blue Earth County, Minnesota

Karen Horn, director of membership and legislative services,
Vermont League of Cities and Towns

Ray Johnson, supervisor, Amador Township,
Chisago County, Minnesota

Steve Kniefel, chairman, Fayal Township,
St. Louis County, Minnesota

Chester Larson, assessor, Liberty Township,
Mountrail County, North Dakota

Jean Paul Lushin, trustee, Center Township,
Marion County, Indiana

Marty Marks, council member, Scotch Plains Township,
Union County, New Jersey

Maxine McClelland, supervisor, Big Rapids Township,
Mecosta County, Michigan

George Mills, retired reporter for the *Des Moines Register*,
Des Moines, Iowa

David Niemeier, treasurer, Blakely Township,
Gage County, Nebraska

George Oster, program manager of research and development,
Fire Service Institute, Iowa State University Extension Service

Robin Reed, information specialist,
Michigan Townships Association

Dennis Rindone, executive secretary,
Town of Princeton, Massachusetts

Bart Russell, executive director,
Connecticut Council of Small Towns

David Russell, director, Intergovernmental Affairs,
Hartford, Connecticut

Val Sawhill, trustee, Coventry Township,
Summit County, Ohio

Cheryl Sharp, treasurer, Cotton Township,
St. Louis County, Minnesota

Bryan E. Smith, executive director,
Township Officials of Illinois

Richard Stadelman, executive director,
Wisconsin Towns Association

Michael Starn, communications manager,
Maine Municipal Association

Amy Sturges, member relations representative,
Pennsylvania League of Cities and Municipalities

Donald Waller, supervisor, Wyoming Township,
Chisago County, Minnesota

Table of Contents

CHAPTER FOUR: Grassroots Government

CHAPTER FIVE: Townships in Today's World

CHAPTER SIX: Townships of the Future

Introduction

DISSEMINATION OF INFORMATION

*Our knowledge is the amassed thought
and experience of innumerable minds.*
—Ralph Waldo Emerson

A few years ago, my oldest daughter was learning about state government in school. I asked her if the discussion included township government and she said no. I told her teacher I would be willing to talk to the class about townships. The teacher was excited about my offer, explaining that she knew very little about township government, and that she had no resources to teach about it. A few days later I spoke to sixth grade classes and the teacher was most appreciative. After hearing my presentation, she said she had the knowledge to teach her students a beginning lesson in township government. It is now a part of that school's curriculum.

Before I was elected a township supervisor, I would not have been able to teach township government. Like my daughter's teacher, I knew very little about it—and I even lived in a township! I knew there was a township board and I knew these elected officials had something to do with the condition of the road in front of my house and the amount of property taxes I paid. I had no idea how many ways these elected officials affected the community in which I lived.

Then one day in late February of 1990, I was asked if I would run against a person who had been an elected official for more than 20 years. The townspeople wanted a change in the township board, but no one had filed to run against the current supervisor. I asked what my duties would be and was told I would need to attend one meeting a month, maybe two, and help "run" the township. Being ignorant about what it meant to run a township, I didn't think it would be too big a job and agreed. A write-in campaign was launched and I won the election on March 13 by a vote of 102 to 61.

Since taking office, I am no longer ignorant about the job of running a township. I have discovered phrases such as public servant, grassroots government, and rural character. I have learned to plan a budget nine months ahead of when I will use it. I can even describe the difference among classes of gravel put on our roads. And I have learned more about the workings of wastewater disposal systems than one can discuss in public. In all, I have been made aware of the numerous needs of my community and how I might be able to serve the people. At first I was frightened and overwhelmed by the responsibilities. Now, it is a great feeling to be making a difference, no matter how small, in my township. Making the correct decisions is not always easy or evident, but being a part of the process is a satisfying reward.

Many other township officials share my feelings of ignorance when first elected to serve the people. Having a book such as this one would have helped me grasp my responsibilities so much quicker, and I would have had a better understanding of the mechanizations of township government. I believe this book will be useful to every township official. Newly elected officials will find the book very helpful, as it will teach the foundations of township government. Other officials will find this book a useful resource for the workings of township government and as a tool to learn how to think in new ways to solve common problems.

Students of local government will find the discussion on townships across our nation very interesting. Townships all began as the foundation of our government, becoming as varied as the faces of our country's residents. Yet through each township, there remains the basic idea of democracy. The nation's townships strive to keep that principle alive.

Township government excites me because it is the form in which our country's founders believed. It is truly government for the people and by the people. I have learned so much on my journey and I am excited at what the future holds. Townships can continue to grow and prosper without adding to our land boundaries. We need to share what we learn with each other, helping to solve problems we are all facing and finding solutions to allow local governments to work together for the better of our communities.

The sharing of information always makes a job easier. It opens the doors to communication and creative thinking—things necessary for townships to work effectively and efficiently. When those things are present, grassroots government is alive in your township.

There are hundreds of opportunities for a township resident, no matter what age, to get involved and help better the community. Some states even allow high school students to be student election judges, offering an up-close look at democracy in action. Unfortunately, most people don't get involved in township government until a decision is made that personally affects their lifestyles or their wallets. I encourage you to not wait to react. Instead, jump in and see how you can make a difference in your community. Help to make your future a better place with the democracy our country's founding fathers intended.

Chapter One

DEFINING TOWNSHIPS

Every man and every body of men on Earth
possess the right of self-government.
　　　　　　　　　—Thomas Jefferson, 1790

TOWNSHIP GOVERNMENT ORIGINS

The founding of our country and the beginnings of township government have something in common: a man named Thomas Jefferson. History has taught us that Jefferson was the primary author of the Declaration of Independence in 1776, which gave the United States freedom from England's rule. It was just a few years later, in 1784, that Jefferson proposed the Northwest Territory Ordinance. Although the ordinance carried the "northwest" description, the land being considered was north of the Ohio River. The territory included what we now refer to as the states of Ohio, Michigan, Indiana, Illinois, Wisconsin, and part of Minnesota.

It was Jefferson's belief that new territories should be self-governing and eventually be admitted to the Union of the original 13 states. In his Northwest Territory Ordinance, he outlined a process to divide land into territories, each with governing authority. These territories would eventually make up 14 new states that would be admitted to the Union. Some people objected to Jefferson's plans because the territories had rectangular boundaries which did not account for natural features such as rivers and mountains. Others objected to the plan because they felt 14 new states were too many and these new states would gain control of Congress.

TOWNSHIP DEFINED IN SIZE

Congress approved Jefferson's ordinance, but it was never put into effect. The governing authority Jefferson envisioned would not come for several years. But Congress was willing to consider Jefferson's ideas; it established the surveying portion of Jefferson's Ordinance. In surveying, Congress began in 1785 to measure the land included in the Northwest Territory by using a system called the Public Land Survey System. Through this measuring came the Land Act of 1796 and the system of townships as we know them today. Most states across the country still have these townships, but only on paper as survey lines, and they are often referred to as geographical townships.

In order to create geographical townships, Congress established by ordinance for land to be divided into squares. Because the eastern lands of the United States had already been settled, the ordinance called for the new surveying to begin in Ohio, near the Ohio River. Surveyors first established a base line, a line running east and west along a line of latitude. From the base line, additional lines were added parallel to the base line in increments of six miles. Next, a principal meridian line was drawn running north and south. Where the principal meridian line intersected the base line, surveyors called that the initial point. From here, lines were added running north and south, also in six-mile increments. These lines were actually lines of longitude. With this pattern of drawing lines, a grid was created of squares measuring six miles on each side. Each square was called a township and each township was assigned an identifying number called a range number. This number identified each township according to its place east or west of the principal meridian. For example, a township might be identified as R2W, meaning it was the second range west of the principal meridian.

This system worked well, except for one problem. Meridian lines all intersect at the poles of the earth, so the six mile increments between the lines on the grid cannot stay exactly six miles apart. The surveyors realized this and made correction lines at approximately every fourth line. You can still see these correction lines today, as some of them follow existing roads. Looking at a map, you can follow a road running north and south that suddenly takes a "jog in the road." This is a correction line. There were also instances when the land was interrupted by a river or a lake, and therefore did not cooperate with the six-square-mile rule of measurement.

For the most part, townships looked alike on a map. The grid created by surveyors resembled a checkerboard, made up of townships six miles square. As difficult as it is to believe, our lives are greatly affected today by these survey lines drawn 200 years ago. These lines still define what form of local government a person will have, what kinds of services that person will have access to, how much taxes a person will pay, and in some states those lines determine which schools children will attend. The lines are invisible and yet they determine so much.

Once surveyors had drawn the lines and established township boundaries, each township was then divided into 36 sections, each section containing a

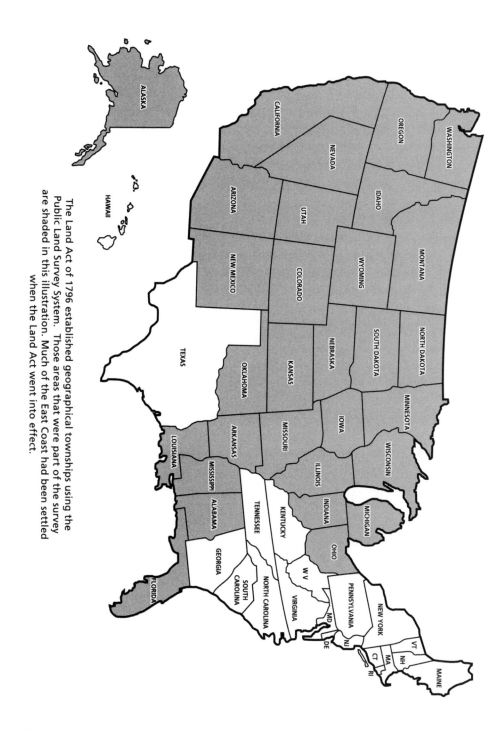

The Land Act of 1796 established geographical townships using the Public Land Survey System. Those areas that were part of the survey are shaded in this illustration. Much of the East Coast had been settled when the Land Act went into effect.

Cambria			Lime	Jamestown
Butternut Valley	Judson	South Bend	Mankato	Le Ray
Lincoln	Garden City	Rapidan	Decoria	McPherson
Ceresco	Vernon Center	Lyra	Beauford	Medo
Pleasant Mound	Shelby	Sterling	Mapleton	Danville

Minnesota River

Le Sueur River

Blue Earth County in southern Minnesota shows a grid of townships, each measuring 6 miles x 6 miles. With two rivers in the northern part of the county, it is easy to see how natural effects of the land create townships with interesting shapes.

square mile, or 640 acres. The ordinance called for the sections to be numbered in a unique way. Each of the sections was given a number from 1 to 36, with the first section located in the northeast corner of a township. The numbers would progress west to the township's border, then drop to the south and progress to the east, and repeat the process. This zigzag form of counting would follow through to the southern border of the township.

The sections were also divided in the hopes that farmers would purchase parcels of land and settle them. Each section was divided into four parts of 160 acres. These parts were called quarters and were referred to as the northeast, northwest, southwest, and southeast. Each quarter could be divided into a north half and a south half, each containing 80 acres. The halves could also be divided in to two 40 acre pieces — the front 40 and the back 40. There are still farmers today who refer to the "back 40" of their property.

All of this explanation helps when looking at a deed for a property. Many times the description is so technical that you can get lost in all of the directions:

> The part of the Southeast Quarter of the Southeast
> Quarter (SE 1/4 of SE 1/4) of Section Thirty-three
> (33), Township Thirty-three (33), Range Twenty-one
> (21), Chisago County, Minnesota described as follows, to-wit:
> Beginning at a point on the South line of said SE 1/4 of SE 1/4,
> 42 feet East of the Southwest corner thereof; thence
> continuing East along said South line for 85 feet; thence
> North, parallel to the West line of said SE 1/4 of SE 1/4 for
> 100 feet; thence West parallel to described first course for
> 85 feet, thence South for 100 feet to the point of beginning.

As mentioned earlier, the eastern United States were already settled when the Public Land Survey System was established. Parts of Ohio were included in the already settled area, but the remaining portion of Ohio had to be surveyed and still fit within the state's boundaries. For that reason, some townships in Ohio measure seven miles square, with 49 sections. Others measured five miles square with only 25 sections. The numbering of sections within the townships vary as well. In some places the numbering starts in the northeast corner of a township going straight south, then moves back up to the north, repeating the process until ending in the southwest corner.

Mention must also be made of the exceptions to the rule. The Public Land Survey System is not found everywhere in the United States. We've already discussed the prior settlement of the eastern states along the Atlantic coast. In addition, when the survey system was developed, parts or all of California, Florida, and Texas were not included. These areas were already settled and some were governed by Spanish rule, using Spain's system of surveying lands.

Cupolas are common on older township buildings, offering an architectural date. Franconia Town Hall in Chisago County, Minnesota was built about 1900. (Ray Johnson)

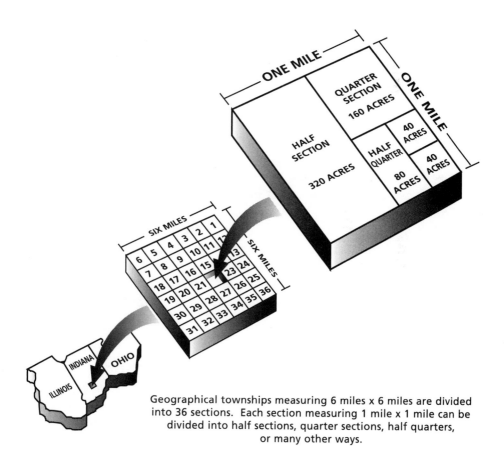

Geographical townships measuring 6 miles x 6 miles are divided into 36 sections. Each section measuring 1 mile x 1 mile can be divided into half sections, quarter sections, half quarters, or many other ways.

Other areas were surveyed using a system called indiscriminate metes and bounds, which uses natural features to describe plots of land.

ESTABLISHING TOWNSHIPS

After land surveying was completed according to the orders by Congress, the next step was to give townships self-governing authority. That came in 1787 when the Northwest Ordinance was passed. This allowed people to become personally involved in governing their territory and protected their right to become members of the Union of original states. The Ordinance established a governor and three judges to rule a territory. Creating township and county government was their first responsibility. The next step was creating a state and being admitted to the Union.

The Northwest Ordinance outlined two steps for a territory to become a state. First, 5,000 free men needed to settle in a territory. These people would then elect officials who would work with the governor and judges of the territory. When there were 60,000 citizens settled in the territory, a request could be made to Congress to make the territory a state of the Union. Once Congress voted and admitted the territory to the Union, it became a state "on equal footing with the original states in all respects whatsoever," as stated in the Ordinance.

Settlers flooded the new territories, and it wasn't long before townships were established and states admitted to the Union. Ohio, in 1803, was the first area of the Northwest Territory to become a state. Following were Indiana in 1816, Illinois in 1818, Michigan in 1837, and Wisconsin in 1848. Only a part of Minnesota was involved in the land of the Northwest Territory, but this area was also settled and eventually the entire state was admitted to the Union in 1858.

SOME STATES DID NOT CHOOSE TOWNSHIP GOVERNMENT

People who live in states that have towns or townships are surprised to find out that only 20 states have this form of government. People who live in states without township government are surprised to learn townships exist. Knowing this, the question arises: Why do only 20 states have township government? I have asked this question for several years and the answer is not an easy one to find. Many people whom I thought should know the answer didn't know. After many hours of research, I arrived at some conclusions.

At the time the early colonies were being settled and governments were being formed, much of the southern and interior land of North America was held by France and Spain. These territories had governments modeled after their mother countries. Similarly, the New England states were established with the English form of town government.

In 1763, the end of the French and Indian War produced an agreement which called for France to give the land known as Canada and all of the territory east of the Mississippi, except for New Orleans, to England. Spain took New Orleans and in exchange gave Florida to England. When the British lost the Revolutionary War in 1783, England accepted the United States' claim to the land between the Appalachian Mountains and the Mississippi River.

During this time, Thomas Jefferson introduced the Northwest Territory Ordinance of 1784, proposing townships and a township form of government for the new territory. Later, in 1803, Thomas Jefferson negotiated the Louisiana Purchase and more land became available. As these territories opened up and were settled, township government expanded out of the New England states.

Not all of the territories were eager to adopt the township form of government. One of the requirements of the Northwest Ordinance prohibited slaves in states created in the Upper Midwest. At this time in the country's history, slavery was a controversial issue. In the North, a free-labor system was used and most people were paid for their work. In the South, a slave-labor system was widely used and a few plantation landowners earned most of the wealth. Many southerners were not eager to adopt the same participatory form of government that the people in the north were using.

The issue of slavery was part of a larger argument about economics. In the southern states, agricultural products were the prime source of revenue. Plantation owners grew tobacco, wheat, and corn, then exported these products to Europe. The South was dependent on slave labor to get these products from the fields to purchasers.

In the northern states, small-scale industries were created to meet the demands of shipping centers along the eastern coast. Rope and sail manufacturers, along with ship builders, formed another layer of businesses such as wholesale traders, commercial services, and insurance brokers. There was economic diversity with fishing, light manufacturing, and farms with crops and animals. Many shops and businesses resulted from the denser population and a broader distribution of wealth. Overall, the types of goods produced in the North not only created jobs, but also stimulated supporting industries. All of these conditions added to the separation of classes between the North and the South.

Division among the people also occurred as a result of land distribution practices. National land policy was strict and not favorable to the average person. Prices were high, with loans difficult to obtain. Many state leaders wanted national land prices to remain high so it would be easier to sell state lands. Still, some states offered land at cheaper prices because there was more land to be had. The country's controlling governmental party at the time did not want to encourage settlers to head west for fear the population would spread too quickly over the land. Thomas Jefferson's Northwest Territory Ordinance helped to solve some of those fears with the controlled development of the available land.

The dividing of land over 200 years ago was complicated and controversial. Leaders were trying to solve current issues, while still allowing for future planning. Some areas organized and became townships, with cities later developing out of the townships. Other areas remained unorganized, with no chosen form of government. It's difficult to believe, but it's true, that some of these unorganized areas still exist today.

One has to wonder if any of the leaders from 200 years ago knew the decisions they made then would affect the way we live today. We must recognize that how we divide land, although still complicated and controversial, will change many aspects of our lives. Altering and moving a government's boundary lines could affect our children's great grandchildren. Annexations are occurring at a rapid rate across the United States as populations increase and each annexation changes survey lines. Cities are looking to townships for land and additional tax base to continue to offer services to their residents. We must be careful in our planning, always conscious of the consequences that will come from altering boundary lines.

Thomas Jefferson had a great vision when he planned the Northwest Territory Ordinance. He worked diligently with Congress to establish survey lines which facilitated the parceling of land. At the same time, he spread the word about the need for a government in the new territory, a government ruled by those same people. The first form of local government was born from a unique way of surveying and dividing land, giving self-governing authority, something city government has never been able to offer taxpayers. Too often today people forget that basic principle when agreeing to let a city annex a part of a township, and in doing so the governing authority is taken away from common citizens and given to elected leaders. We cannot lose sight of the fact that township government is set up and is ready, willing, and able to do the work the people demand.

An aerial viewpoint emphasizes the division of land by agricultural use, commercial and residential areas, and road systems. (Mart Aerial Photography, Minnesota Historical Society)

Chapter Two
CHAIN OF COMMAND

In this world of dramatic change, one of the biggest obstacles to our changing is the machinery of government itself. It's frankly been stuck in the past, wasting too much money, often ignoring the taxpayer, coping with outdated systems and archaic technology, and most of all, eroding the confidence of the American people that government can make change work for them.
—President Bill Clinton, September 1993

LET'S START AT THE BEGINNING

History teachers all across the country have done an excellent job over the years teaching our country's chain of command, beginning with the president and vice president. Each of us learned throughout grade school and high school that our country's government has three branches. At some point we were taught the functions of these government branches, but if tested on the topic today most of us would do a poor job. To refresh our memories and to understand the workings of township government, a discussion on the hierarchy of government is in order.

Long before our country's government was imagined, even before the Pilgrims disembarked from the *Mayflower*, a form of government was established called the Mayflower Compact. The Pilgrims had no authority to make or enforce rules in their new land, but they knew that without rules their society would collapse. The men signed an agreement before they left the ship that called for general laws for the good of the people. It was an informal agreement, but it helped establish the idea of government by the people.

TOWNSHIP GOVERNMENT

As our country was settled, territories were established and each created a form of government to manage its affairs. Small governmental units were founded across the colonies as states began to form. The oldest form of government in the United States is that of township government. It was first established in Rhode Island in 1636, in place even before the idea of statehood. New England towns adopted this form of local government, incorporating town meetings and the election of citizens to town boards.

As time passed, conflicts grew within colonies; England tried to retain its rule over the new land. Battles were fought over new territories between England and France, and England and Spain, while settlers in the new colonies wanted their own form of government.

In 1754, Benjamin Franklin was among a group of leaders who attended a meeting in Albany, New York which came to be called the Albany Congress. Leaders of the American colonies met with Native Americans to strengthen ties in preparation for war with France. The Haudenosaunee, known as the Six Nations Iroquois Confederacy, had a form of government that appealed to Franklin. He and several colonists later sat in on treaty council meetings and became knowledgeable in native customs and the Iroquois constitution. There is a growing number of historians who believe Franklin was influenced by the Haudenosaunee democracy and brought its concept to discussions as our country's constitution was drafted.

The process of writing the constitution was long and complicated, but the outcome was well worth the efforts of many. The Declaration of Independence, written and adopted in 1776, solidified the fight for freedom and liberty for the colonies. Once England agreed to peace terms and accepted the independence of the thirteen colonies, a framework was needed for the United States government and the Articles of Confederation were written. Within three years, twelve of the colonies, now states, approved the Articles. Maryland chose to holdout, disputing the ownership of western lands fought for by the thirteen states.

A NEW GOVERNMENT

In September 1786, delegates from nine states agreed to gather for a convention to discuss concerns about trade disputes, but only five states were represented at the convention. Alexander Hamilton, one of the delegates, drafted a letter urging all states to send representatives to a convention to be held in Philadelphia in May 1787. Hamilton wanted to discuss more than just trade disputes. He wanted to revise the Articles of Confederation.

After much persuasion, every state except Rhode Island sent representatives to the convention held in May. In all, 55 delegates gathered, adopted procedures for the meeting, chose George Washington as the presiding officer, and voted to close the doors to conduct the remainder of the convention in secret. These delegates were some of the most educated men in America. Many of them had been members of their state legislatures and had helped write their state constitutions. Some of the delegates were farmers, doctors, or business owners. About half were lawyers. Over time, they came to be known as the founding fathers of our country.

Just a few days after the convention began, Edmund Randolph introduced a document titled "The Virginia Plan," written by James Madison. This document outlined a new national government made up of three branches including a congress with two houses. Delegates argued the basic principles of this document for many days. The most heated argument centered on whether members of congress should be elected by the citizens of each state, or if citizens would elect members of one house and then those members would appoint the members of the other house. Madison argued that for a government to be free, the people must be able to elect their representatives.

Another debate unresolved for weeks involved whether states should be represented in Congress based on populations. Small states were opposed to this as they would only have one representative. Northern states began to argue with southern states over trade issues and slavery. Compromises were discussed often, but the debates continued.

Months passed with arguments on countless issues affecting all of the states. The business of a new government was a serious one, and every delegate involved wanted to do the right thing for the people being represented. Finally a document was written on which the delegates could agree, full of compromises between large states and small, between states in the north and states in the south. On September 17, 1787, forty-two of the delegates remained and thirty-nine of them signed the Constitution. The summer had been long and difficult, but their work was done and they went home to persuade their people to accept this constitution.

Some people feared the document, calling it too radical. These people believed a strong national government would ruin any chances of states having their own governments. States' rights versus a constitutional government was a common debate. There were also fears that government would endanger individual liberties without a bill of rights. Still, other people believed states were represented equally and fairly by leaders the citizens would elect. The task was not easy, but it took less than a year from the time the document left Congress to get the necessary approval of nine out of thirteen states. By 1790, all thirteen states had ratified the document.

THE FEDERAL GOVERNMENT

Adopted in 1789, the Constitution outlined the structure of our country's government and how to operate it. Avoiding the monarchy form of government from England and foreign dictatorships, the Constitution called for three branches of government: executive, legislative, and judicial. The executive branch consists of the office of president and vice president, and includes the executive departments, also known as the cabinet. Some departments are more well known than others, such as The Department of Justice, The Department of Defense, The Department of State, The Department of Agriculture, and The Department of Education. There are fourteen departments in all, each created by congress to allow for efficient and effective governing of specific affairs. In addition to the departments, there are several organizations that come under the heading of the executive branch. These include the White House staff, the National Security Council, and many others. Each department of the executive branch of government employs thousands of workers, making the government our country's largest employer.

The legislative branch of the government is also called a bicameral congress, meaning there are two chambers, the Senate and the House of Representatives. This is the branch of national government most Americans relate to because of the familiarity we have with the people we elect to represent us. The writers of our country's constitution believed separate groups would provide a system of checks and balances, insuring protection against the abuse of power. Balance would be established between the power of the states and nation (in the Senate) against the power of the people (in the House). The idea was that if both groups must approve every law, then laws would be well thought out and argued carefully. Decisions would not be made carelessly or for the good of a select few. Both houses of Congress have many duties, some of which allow for the power to levy and collect taxes, to provide for armed forces, to declare war, and to introduce laws necessary to abide by our country's constitution.

The senate is made up of 100 members, with each state represented by two senators. They are elected in even-numbered years for a term of six years. It follows, then, that one-third of the senate is up for re-election every other year. The positive side of that equation is that two-thirds of the senate remains with some legislative experience to help guide new members.

Things get more complicated with the House of Representatives. Here a formula is used based on a state's population. Each state is divided into districts, each district representing about 530,000 persons, and each district elects one representative to the House. Every two years a district elects a representative for a two-year term. Currently, seven states have low populations

On average, there are three to five million visitors every year to the nation's capital building. (Monica Dwyer Abress)

allowing only one member in the House of Representatives. These states are: Alaska, Delaware, Montana, North Dakota, South Dakota, Vermont, and Wyoming. Likewise, the densely populated states have the most representatives. At present, there are six states with 20 representatives or more. California leads the list with 52. The other five states are: Florida, Illinois, New York, Pennsylvania, and Texas.

Every ten years, the constitution calls for a nationwide census to occur, updating current state populations. As a result, there is often the need for a change in district lines to keep districts equal and as close to the 530,000 population as possible. We can expect alterations in these districts reflecting the change in population patterns once results of the 2000 census are announced.

In some countries, legislative officials are appointed by a country's leader and the legislature shows little diversity. Since each member of our country's congress is elected by the residents of his or her state, there is a large variety of beliefs and lifestyles reflecting the faces of our country. Some are members of the Republican Party, some from the Democratic Party, and a growing number are coming in with ties to the Reform Party and the Independent Party, even the Socialist Party. Our congress is not a hierarchy as in some countries; instead its power is distributed equally among the states and the people.

The third branch of our country's government is the judicial branch. Led by the United States Supreme Court, this is a system of courts spread throughout our country. As a whole, the United States is divided into federal judicial districts making up 11 courts of appeals and 91 district courts. These districts are based on population and the number of cases being presented. Congress has the right to redefine the boundaries of the districts and may do so after the 2000 census. The purpose of these courts is to protect and interpret the laws established in the Constitution, to deal with cases involving foreign countries or diplomats from foreign countries, and to handle disagreements between states. Unlike the elected members of congress, federal judges hold office until they resign, retire, or die.

STATE REGIMES

The writers of our country's constitution realized that each state must have its own form of government. The Tenth Amendment to the constitution states, "The powers not delegated to the United States by the Constitution, nor prohibited by it to the states, are reserved to the states respectively, or to the people." It was efficient for the country's federal government to be in charge of major concerns, for example defense and foreign relations. However, the belief was that each state would be better attuned to the needs of its own residents, when concerning matters of providing and regulating transportation, education, police and fire protection, and medical services.

There are many times when the needs of the residents of a state overlap with the needs of the country. It is then that the federal Congress does its work of introducing and passing laws or changing existing laws for the good of the country. But for the most part, states are allowed to rule themselves, provided they pass no laws which contradict or violate the United States Constitution or any United States laws and treaties.

Like the national government, states have three branches of government carrying the same names — legislative, executive, and judicial — performing the same functions, but with a state focus. Just as the country has a president and vice president for leaders, states have a governor and almost all states have a lieutenant governor. Each state also has its own congress comprised of an upper house called the Senate and a lower house called the House of Representatives, House of Delegates, or the General Assembly. Nebraska is the only state that makes exception to this, as that state has a single legislative body.

Each state is divided into districts based on population, and each district is represented by senators and representatives. Some states refer to representatives as delegates. In Wisconsin, they are assemblymen. In most states, the senators serve a term of four years and the representatives serve two-year terms.

Each state has its own constitution, modeled after the federal constitution, containing a plan for the organization of the state's government and a statement of rights for its people. In many respects a state's constitution is more detailed than the federal one, dealing specifically with laws set forth to manage all of a state's affairs and providing for the rights of its people.

COUNTY ADMINISTRATIONS

Just as the authors of our country's constitution recognized the need for state government, the need for smaller, more localized governmental units was also acknowledged. As states were divided into congressional and judicial districts, they were also divided into counties. Most counties in the United States contain two or more townships and several villages or cities. There are exceptions to this rule. New York City is so large that it is divided into five boroughs, each acting as a county. You've heard these areas referred to as The Bronx, Brooklyn, Manhattan, Queens, and Staten Island. In contrast, Arlington County, Virginia is one continuous suburban area located across the Potomac River from Washington, D.C. It contains no townships or cities. Similarly, Denver County in Colorado shares the same boundary lines with the city of Denver and has no county government, even though the rest of the state relies on the county form of government. The same applies to the city of Jacksonville, Florida in Duval County. There are two states in which a county form of government is used, but under a different name: Alaska has boroughs, Louisiana has parishes.

Most counties across the United States act as a governing authority. There are three states, however, in which the county has little role. In Rhode Island and Vermont, the counties are merely tools to divide judicial districts. Local government falls to the cities, villages, towns, and townships. The state of Connecticut voted in 1960 to abolish county government and no longer has counties. Many New England states have county governments which perform limited functions.

For counties that have governing authority, there are three forms of leadership. First and most common is a commission led by a board of commissioners or supervisors, each elected by the county's residents. In Louisiana, commission members are called parish police jurors. In New Jersey, county government is a board of chosen freeholders.

A second form of county government is that of a commission with an administrator. Under this form, a board of commissioners is elected by the county residents, and the board in turn appoints an administrator. Often the administrator has the authority to hire and fire employees and is responsible for planning the county's budget.

The third form of county government involves an elected council with an executive administrative officer. This officer has the authority to hire and fire employees, and authority extends to the power to veto ordinances (local laws) adopted by the council. In recent years, more states have chosen the administrator or executive officer form of county government.

Typically, in larger counties of each state, districts are formed based on populations; one commissioner is elected to represent one district. Meanwhile, in smaller counties, boards are elected as a whole by the residents of the entire county.

Just as the federal government oversees the state governments, each state government oversees its county governments. Again, there is an overlapping of some services, but efficiency in all of the commissioners' duties is called for by voters at election time. Since each state must abide by the constitutional laws of the United States, so must each county abide by its state's constitution, passing no laws that contradict or violate.

For the most part, a county government functions as a local outlet of state government for its defined territory. State government serves a large area and deals with major policies. County government serves a smaller area, meeting the needs for courts, jails, and in some states health and welfare services. A large concern of county government is the responsibility it has to build and maintain roads, and the need to levy tax to support that responsibility. Another major concern is the management of county planning and zoning regulations. In recent years, planning and zoning issues have become extremely controversial as rural areas deal with urban sprawl and population growth and decline. Many cities and townships, where allowed by state law, now manage their own planning and zoning. These communities like the local control allowed, and the authority to manage their land to be vested in their locally elected officials. Many residents believe local officials know and understand the planning and zoning issues much better than county officials, who may reside in other communities within the county or somewhere else in the state.

CITY COUNCILS

As the hierarchy of government makes its way down to cities, the civics lesson becomes much more complicated. Part of the problem is definitions. Not all cities are cities. There are several names used to define local governments. "Towns" usually refers to the colonial New England form of government, which still exists today. Many of these towns are actually municipalities and function as major cities. However, in some states, such as Wisconsin, "towns" are equivalent to Midwestern "townships." Many other states use the term town interchangeably with "city" and "village" to describe local municipalities.

As county government serves the people scattered over a large area within a state, city government must meet the needs of a small, localized area. State laws give cities the necessary authority to provide for a concentrated population, coordinating services on a daily basis. Directly serving the needs of the people, cities provide most of the services required, be they police and fire protection, affordable housing, or sewer and water systems, to name a few. While city governments vary across the United States, whether large or small, all cities have some kind of city council elected by the voters.

The oldest form of city government is that of a mayor with a council, a form once used by nearly all cities in the United States. This form allows the council to pass city ordinances and laws, adopt a budget and set property tax rates, and oversee the managing of the city's needs. Oftentimes the mayor is responsible for the hiring and firing of the leaders of the city's departments. The mayor may also have the power of veto over city ordinances and is frequently responsible for the drafting of a city's budget.

Because an elected official is usually considered a part-time job, more cities are hiring a full-time city manager who is under the direction of the city council. This council-manager form of government allows cities to hire an expert in management, crucial to the needs of today's complex urban problems. With this form of government, the city council sets city policy and passes ordinances, and the city manager sees that the council's decisions are carried out. The city manager is responsible for drafting the city's budget and overseeing the city's departments. Under this form of government, the manager is hired by the council, not elected by the people. As long as the manager fulfills the duties of the office, in a satisfactory manner according to the council, the manager will keep the job.

Another, less well-known form of city government, is called a commission form of government. Not used by many cities, here a council is responsible for all of the duties of the city. Usually the council is made up of three members, sometimes more, each with equal voting authority. Each council member supervises a city department and one member acts as a chairperson for the purpose of conducting meetings. Generally this form of government is found in very small, rural cities and villages.

TOWNSHIP BOARDS

Township government, the oldest form of government and the foundation of our government, is very much in existence today. Township boards meet in small township halls or in large community centers, working with the townspeople, for the townspeople. Each state with the traditional form of township government holds elections in which the local voters choose officers to manage each township. These same electors attend an annual meeting, at which the townspeople determine the amount of tax burden placed upon themselves and decide where that money will be spent. Unlike townships, most other local governments hold hearings to discuss budgets, with the final decisions made by the local officials. Township government gives the financial authority to the taxpayers. This is unique in that no other form of government gives the people so much power.

There are 20 states that have the township form of government in three regions of the United States. In New England, towns or townships are found in Connecticut, Maine, Massachusetts, New Hampshire, Rhode Island, and Vermont. New Jersey and Pennsylvania are the Mid-Atlantic states with towns or townships. The Midwest states with towns or townships are Illinois, Indiana, Iowa, Kansas, Michigan, Minnesota, Missouri, Nebraska, North Dakota, Ohio, South Dakota, and Wisconsin.

Built in 1861, the Sunrise Township Hall in Chisago County, Minnesota is the oldest public building in the state that is still in use. (Ray Johnson)

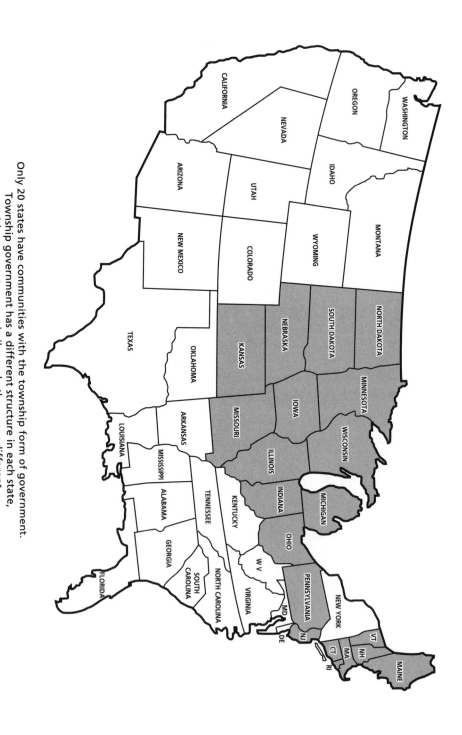

Only 20 states have communities with the township form of government. Township government has a different structure in each state, with some states very similar and others very different.

Chapter Three
MAGNIFYING DIFFERENCES

The framers of the Constitution well understood that each locality, having separate and distinct interests, required separate and distinct laws, domestic institutions, and police regulations adapted to its own wants and its own condition; and they acted on the presumption, also, that these laws and institutions would be as diversified and as dissimilar as the States would be numerous and that no two would be precisely alike, because the interests of no two would be precisely the same.
　　　　–Stephen A. Douglas, 1858, presidential candidate running against Abraham Lincoln

COMPARISONS

Townships began as squares containing 36 square miles. But as populations grew, some townships were made even smaller when a city formed inside the boundaries of a township. Many townships across the country have sections carved out for city limits. On a plat map a township may take the shape of a six miles by six miles square, but not possess the full 36 square miles within that square. Over the years many cities have grown and expanded their limits, consuming land within townships. Some township governments have been swallowed completely, merging with cities and disappearing from the map altogether.

As townships evolved, they took on different looks in various states. Communities changed in beliefs and new laws were passed. Many parts of the country developed rapidly, with some states creating largely populated townships to have many governing responsibilities. For other areas, especially the Midwest, the land has stayed in agricultural uses and populations remain small. No two townships are exactly alike, but similarities abound. Based on the democratic foundation of America, township government acts efficiently, quietly going about its job. Every township has a board of supervisors, trustees, or selectmen that manages the day-to-day business of running a township. Following James Madison's argument that, for a government to be free the people must be able to elect their representatives, each member of the board is elected by the residents of a township.

In most states where organized townships exist, townspeople gather for the all-important annual meeting to vote on the operating budget for the next year. In essence they are determining their own tax burden. For smaller townships, the day-to-day management is not without problems, but generally not too difficult. For larger townships, the services being provided to the townspeople require many employees and many management decisions.

Following is a comparison of each of the 20 states that have the township form of government. Each state is briefly discussed to give a perspective on similarities and differences among all 20. At the end of the chapter there is a chart that offers another opportunity for comparison.

CONNECTICUT

The state of Connecticut has 169 municipalities, of which 108 are chartered towns. The rest are nonchartered towns. There are 94 towns that have a board of selectmen and use the township meeting form of government.

In 1960, county government was abolished in this state and towns have complete governing authority. Along with complete authority comes a long list of responsibilities: police and fire protection, road and bridge maintenance, planning and zoning, and water and sewer to name a few.

As mentioned previously, the state of Connecticut has two types of towns, charter and noncharter. There is no set of standards, such as size of population, to make a charter town. A town is chartered only because the town has adopted a charter (a specific set of ordinances or laws). There is no difference between the two types of towns in a legal sense and no difference in powers. A nonchartered town is guided by state statutes in how it is organized. Usually these towns have a smaller population and have a three- or five-member board of selectmen. Every two years the entire board is up for re-election.

A charter town can be organized differently if electors desire, with a town manager form of government and a council with more authority over finances. Generally towns with larger populations vote to adopt a charter government.

As towns become more urban, many town meeting functions in charter towns are being delegated to the board.

ILLINOIS

There are 1,433 townships in the state of Illinois serving more than eight million people. Most townships elect eight officials to serve their residents: supervisor, clerk, four trustees, assessor, and highway commissioner. A township board of trustees is made up of a supervisor, four trustees, and a clerk. The supervisor is chief executive officer of the township, chair of the township board of trustees, supervisor of general assistance, and treasurer of all township funds and road district funds. The board of trustees is the legislative branch of township government, responsible for the township's policies. A township clerk serves as clerk of the board of trustees, clerk of the road district, the local election authority, and the keeper of all township records except for general assistance case records. When decisions are made, the supervisor and each trustee have one vote. The clerk does not have a vote. All officials are elected to a four-year term with no elections staggered, making it possible to have a completely new board after an election.

For smaller townships, those with less than four miles of road, the township board manages the roads, often contracting for road maintenance with a city, private contractor, or by an intergovernmental agreement. When a township has more than four miles of road, the highway commissioner is responsible for maintaining all of the township's roads and bridges. Currently, 53 percent of the state's road miles are under the jurisdiction of township road districts. The highway commissioner sets his/her own policies and prioritizes the necessary road maintenance. The commissioner prepares the road budget and the township board approves it. The road commissioner's budget is separate from the township's budget, and the road commissioner has authority to levy a tax for road expenses. Many people believe the road commissioner holds a lot of power because he/she answers only to the voting public. But the responsibilities are great and Mother Nature can cause many problems, the consequence of which is getting voted out of office for poor job performance.

Citizens also elect an assessor who establishes property values on all land parcels in the township. An assessor is required by law to have formal training before running for office. Even though the assessor establishes property values, the assessor does not levy the taxes. The power to levy a tax is with the township board. The tax levy amount is also affected by school districts and other governments which can levy taxes for services against the values determined by the assessor.

Illinois townships are mandated to provide general assistance, property assessment, and maintain roads and bridges. Many townships also provide other services, including health and emergency services; environmental services; youth programming; programs designed for disabled citizens and senior citizens; and relief assistance.

INDIANA

The state of Indiana has 1,008 townships. Elections are held every four years in November. All terms expire at the same time making it possible to have an entirely new elected board. Township residents elect a trustee and three township board members. The trustee is the chief administrative officer of the township and performs many duties: he/she prepares the annual budget for township board approval, is responsible for poor relief and the records of such relief, provides fire protection, is responsible for the eradication of weeds, issues licenses for dogs, keeps records of the township's official proceedings, receives and disburses all monies belonging to the township, supervises the care of abandoned cemeteries in the township, and serves as "park governor" for township parks. In some counties, the trustee also serves as administrator for township schools. In townships with populations of less than 5,000, the trustee has the duties of assessor. For townships with populations of 5,000 to 8,000, an assessor may be elected if the people do not want the trustee to have that duty. Townships with populations greater than 8,000 are mandated to have separate positions of trustee and assessor.

The township board members adopt the annual budget, authorize the incurring of indebtedness, serve as a township board of finance, and assign salaries to township officials. The township board also determines and imposes tax levies. However, the total of all levies is set by the state board of tax commissioners.

In 1993, Indiana townships were allowed by legislative action to govern themselves "absent legal restrictions." This means that the legislature gave townships the right to exercise any power not expressly denied them, nor granted to another government entity. However, townships are not allowed to adopt an ordinance, impose a penalty, require a license fee, or impose a service charge or user fee unless authorized by state statute.

IOWA

Township boards in Iowa resemble those of other states, but their powers are limited. Elected are a clerk and three trustees, each serving for a term of four years. There are no roads maintained by townships, as the counties take care of those duties. The county board of supervisors establishes the compensation for trustees and trustees are then paid by the county.

In the late 1800s, townships played an important role in Iowa. Townships were active local governments, involved in the maintenance of roads, in

Building a road used to be a monumental task. The first step often involved clearing brush and trees from heavily wooded areas. (1935, Minnesota Historical Society)

The back-breaking work continued as a road bed was established. This photo was taken at the same site 9 days after the previously shown brush clearing photo. (1935, Minnesota Historical Society)

administering schools, in establishing and maintaining cemeteries, and as overseers of the poor.

Around 1940, the state took a severe financial punishment from the depression of the 1930s and from the effects of the Dust Bowl. Counties were very poor and townships could not continue to operate on their small budgets. Population losses made it too costly for local governments to continue to maintain roads and provide services. By 1975, the township boundaries remained as districts, but the majority of powers township boards were authorized to use disappeared. County boards believed they were the most efficient level of government and transferred duties from townships to counties, placing more emphasis on developing cities.

There are 1,588 townships still in existence in Iowa, but their roles in the community are limited. The main purposes of township governments today are to provide fire protection, to manage township cemeteries, and to assist in fence viewing. As fence viewers, officials are called upon to negotiate the maintenance of fences that keep livestock within their bounds.

Providing fire protection is mandated and the state sets a maximum levy amount for this purpose. However, township budgets are small and often townships work with cities for joint powers agreements in providing fire service. Because this has created a great deal of tension between the local governments, measures are being taken to improve communication and cooperation among cities, townships, and fire departments. Townships are allowed an unlimited levy amount to maintain, improve, and manage township cemeteries. The duties and responsibilities are many, as state law clearly defines the management of cemeteries.

KANSAS

The state of Kansas has 1,541 townships and each elects a trustee, clerk, and treasurer. These three members make up the township board, and each is elected to a four-year term. The terms are staggered, allowing for incumbents to help a smooth transition when a new member is elected. The township trustee divides the township into road districts and a road overseer is elected. Kansas township boards work with the boards of county commissioners to determine budgets and to levy property taxes in the township for township roads and other business. If the trustee and the county commissioners fail to agree on a levy, the county commissioners shall levy the tax. Each township trustee, clerk, and treasurer make up an auditing board, which is mandated to meet four times each year to examine and audit all claims against the township. An annual report of all claims against the township must be filed with the county clerk for approval by the county commissioners.

Townships in the eastern part of the state do not hold many meetings and their responsibilities are few. In this part of the state there are many cities and the county provides many of the services. These townships basically provide supplemental road work for the county. In the western part of the state, the counties are physically very large and there are not many incorporated cities. Here the townships provide many services and their responsibilities are numerous.

MAINE

The state of Maine has four forms of municipalities: city, town, plantation, and Indian nation. There are nearly 500 municipalities in the state, of which only 22 are cities. Almost 90 percent of the municipalities have the town meeting form of government. The town board of selectmen is the most common administration in towns, however some larger towns have hired an administrative assistant to help with some of the board's duties. Others have hired a town manager. The difference between a town manager and an administrative assistant is not in the duties they perform, but in the source and degree of authority each has.

Maine is a "home rule" state, allowing towns to enact laws, providing such ordinances do not go against the state's laws or constitution. This gives towns the authority to pass ordinances that govern all aspects of the community.

State statutes call for a town board to have a minimum of three members. Some towns have chosen by charter or by ordinance to have five or seven selectmen. Elections are in the spring for most towns and most terms for selectmen are for only one year. Many towns have enacted ordinances to allow for staggered terms, and some ordinances allow for two- or three-year terms. However, the majority of communities still have only one-year terms. Town boards oversee many municipal services, such as road construction and maintenance, water and sewer, police and fire protection, land use planning, welfare, and public education. Townspeople also may choose to elect or appoint a town clerk, tax collector, road commissioner, board of assessors, and overseers of the poor.

Maine has four different types of school systems, one of which is administered by the local municipality. For towns that belong to a school district, the town's share of the school budget is billed to the town. When the town's budget is planned, the town board includes this amount in the town's budget, and the townspeople approve the total budget for the town.

MASSACHUSETTS

Towns in Massachusetts are governed by a board of selectmen whose elections are held for three-year terms. Those terms are staggered so there is always an incumbent on the board. Smaller towns have boards of three selectmen, while

Once a road is built, maintenance requires reshaping to deal with frost boils and to keep ditches open for proper drainage of rain and snow. The work done by men with shovels was a test of strength and perseverance. (circa 1940, Minnesota Historical Society)

larger towns have five selectmen. Some larger towns also hire a chief municipal officer to oversee the management of day-to-day operations. The state has 303 towns, each holding an annual meeting in the spring. Besides the selectmen, a moderator is elected for a term of one or three years. His or her duty is to preside over all proceedings. Towns also elect a clerk for a term of one or more years, or in some towns the clerk is an appointed position. In recent years, some towns have gone to a representative form of government.

All towns provide many municipal services for the residents, including road maintenance, water and sewer service, and police and fire protection. Compared to most states, county government has a very diminished role in Massachusetts. Municipalities must provide most of the services or arrange for services through intergovernmental agreements.

At one time it was mandatory for all landowners to attend the annual meeting. Citizens who did not attend were fined. That law changed many years ago, and attendance at town meetings has decreased. Still, voters have the right to elect the officers, set salaries for paid positions, vote to appropriate money for the operation of the town's business, and adopt local statutes or by-laws. Massachusetts towns are also allowed at an annual meeting to appropriate five percent of the previous year's levy for a reserve fund for extraordinary expenditures.

MICHIGAN

There are 1,242 townships in Michigan serving more than 41 percent of the state's residents. Township boards consist of a supervisor, two or four trustees (depending on population), clerk, and treasurer. Each of these officials is elected to a four-year term, with elections held in November, at the same time as presidential elections.

The state's Township Zoning Act gives township boards broad powers to enact and enforce ordinances. The township board also adopts an annual budget and tax levy. The township supervisor moderates meetings, ensures that property tax assessments conform to state laws, and oversees the day-to-day functions of the township. In recent years, some townships have hired a manager to look after daily operations. The township clerk manages all township records, accounts for township finances, and oversees elections conducted by the township. The treasurer collects property taxes for the township, schools, the county, and other tax-levying entities. State law mandates Michigan townships to collect taxes, conduct elections, and perform assessment administration.

In recent years, many townships have voted to no longer hold an annual meeting. Adopting the township's budget is by the township board's vote, not the people's.

Michigan townships do not have responsibility to maintain roads, as this is a county government function. However, many townships levy extra taxes and expend general fund monies to repair and construct roads. In many areas, township residents are not happy with the way the counties are handling the road maintenance and want to have greater control. There is a growing energy to create new legislation to change the method in which roads are maintained.

Many townships provide water and sewer service, police and fire protection, emergency medical services, and recreational programs. Townships are allowed to pass ordinances, including zoning ordinances regulating land use. Michigan law provides for the detachment of land from a city back to a township, something many states do not allow.

The state of Michigan has two types of townships: general law and charter. General law townships are smaller in population, are required to hold township board meetings at least quarterly, and are allowed by state statute to levy 1 mill for general township operations. (A mill rate, or tax rate, is a formula used in some states to determine tax assessed value of property. One mill equals one-tenth of a cent, or $.001.)

Charter township status is a special classification created in 1947 by Michigan legislation allowing additional powers, greater protection against annexation by a city, and streamlined administration. A township may become a charter township by a board resolution, but higher taxation authority is not given to the charter unless a special township election approves the charter. Charter townships are required to meet at least monthly. If charter status is approved at an election, the charter township can levy up to 5 mills for township operations without further voter approval, and can levy an additional five mills with voter approval.

MINNESOTA

There are 1,793 townships in Minnesota serving almost 902,000 residents. Township boards are comprised of three to five supervisors, a clerk, and a treasurer. Almost all township elections are held the second Tuesday in March, and the treasurer and clerk are elected for terms of two years, although these positions may be appointed if townships so choose. Townships may also vote to combine the positions of clerk and treasurer into one. Supervisors are elected to three-year terms. All terms are staggered (except when there are five person boards), so only one supervisor is up for election each year.

The three supervisors choose one to act as the chairperson of the township board. He or she moderates meetings and oversees the daily operations. The supervisors act as the township legislative branch, responsible for all township policies and affairs of the township. The township board members establish budgets, with townspeople adopting the levy at annual meetings held in

March. The township board authorizes the incurring of indebtedness, serves as a township board of audit, and assigns salaries to township officials. The township board can pass ordinances and it can adopt land use and zoning regulations and restrictions in the township. The township board may appoint a town administrator, responsible for the administration and supervision of the township's operations.

The township clerk manages all township records, records minutes of all proceedings, accounts for township finances, and oversees elections conducted by the township. The treasurer receives and takes charge of all money belonging to the township, keeping accurate records of all transactions.

Minnesota townships are responsible for the road and bridge maintenance of all township roads. The state has approximately 56,000 miles of township roads with 6,000 bridges, comprising 43 percent of total road miles in Minnesota. Some townships provide water and sewer service, police and fire protection, emergency medical services, and recreational programs.

MISSOURI

Researching information on township government in Missouri has proved a challenge. There is no association for townships and although the Missouri Association of Counties oversees townships, the organization has very little information about them. No one could offer either a list of elected township officials or population numbers.

There are 114 counties in Missouri and of those 23 have communities that operate under the township form of government. All are located in the northern part of the state. The other 91 counties have townships that exist only as geographical areas. In each township with the township form of government, there is a board of trustees made up of five members. Two are trustees, one is a combination treasurer and trustee, one is a clerk, and one is a tax collector. Only the two trustees and the treasurer/trustee are voting members of the board. Elections are held in April, with terms of all officers lasting two years. The terms are not staggered, so it is possible to elect an entirely new township board in an election.

Townships in Missouri serve one purpose, and that is to take care of all roads. The townships do not have a budget; money for road maintenance comes from the county. Several times in the last 20 years counties have tried to abolish townships. But residents have not allowed it. Local control of the roads is very popular and township residents won't give that up. The Missouri General Assembly could pass legislation to eliminate townships, but that is unlikely. The legislature was successful, however, in eliminating the township assessor position in the early 1980s.

These farmers used horses to make the work easier while building a farm-to-market road, a road used to transport crops. (1936, Minnesota Historical Society)

NEBRASKA

Information on township government in Nebraska is difficult to find. Township government exists in only 28 of Nebraska's 93 counties. There are about 450 townships in the state and each elects three township officials: a chairperson, a secretary/clerk, and a treasurer. Each is elected to a four-year term, and terms run together so it is possible to have a completely new board elected in the same election.

Township boards used to prepare the annual budget and present it to the townspeople for their approval. But the state legislature changed this process and now the township board presents the budget to the county board of supervisors (or commissioners in more populated counties). Each township officer is currently paid $250 a year for performing the duties of office.

Townships provide all maintenance of the roads and every township has its own road equipment. Every year the county allocates funds to each township for nine miles of gravel, and township boards decide where to spread it. Townships are responsible for maintaining smaller ditches and culverts smaller than 48 inches. Road signs are installed by the county, but townships pay for half of the cost.

Municipal services are too costly for the townships to provide. Fire protection is provided through fire districts, established through intergovernmental cooperation.

NEW HAMPSHIRE

In its early history, New Hampshire was under England's rule and many of the lands were purchased from and by the signature of the King. Towns were established because this was the form of government used in England. Today New Hampshire has 234 municipalities. Of those, 219 have the township form of government. County government exists in this state, but township government is the base and holds most of the power.

New Hampshire towns are governed by a board of selectmen, each elected for a term of three years, with elections staggered. Most towns have three selectmen, although more towns are going to a board of five selectmen. Town clerks serve a three-year term, as do treasurers. Townspeople elect a moderator to a two-year term, whose duties include facilitating town meetings. By law, the selectmen make up the board of assessors. However, most towns hire a full-time assessor or a consulting firm whose yearly compensation may be determined by the voters of the town at the annual meeting. Some towns hire a manager to oversee the town's daily operations while others rely on a town administrator or administrative assistant.

Municipal services provided by towns include maintenance of roads and bridges, police and fire protection, water and sewer systems, park maintenance, cemetery maintenance, and poor relief administration. New Hampshire towns are mandated to maintain membership in three organizations: New Hampshire Association of Assessing Officials, New Hampshire City and Town Clerks' Association, and the New Hampshire Tax Collectors' Association. Voluntarily, there is 100 percent membership of towns in the New Hampshire Municipal Association.

NEW JERSEY

New Jersey has 12 major forms of government, one of which is the township form. There are 233 municipalities with "township" in their name, but only 147 of these follow the township form of government. Townships are served by committees comprised of three or five council members, each elected to a term of four years, with elections staggered. Elections are held every two years in odd-numbered years. Three members are elected at one election to serve four years. Two members are elected at the next council election (two years later), also to serve four years.

One member of the committee is chosen by the others to act as mayor, serving in that capacity for one year. The mayor, whose official title is chairman of the township committee, presides over the meetings but has no veto power or other special powers. The committee appoints an attorney, treasurer, engineer, tax collector, tax assessor, and police chief. Most townships hire a manager for daily operations.

By law, every municipality in New Jersey must have a municipal clerk who is usually appointed to a three-year term. The municipal clerk is the top administrative official in the township, managing much of the business of operating the township. The clerk administers all policies passed by the committee and all official communications are sent with the clerk's signature. The clerk is responsible for setting agendas for committee meetings and keeping the records of all meeting minutes. The clerk is also the registrar of vital statistics and secretary to the board of health. All birth, death, and marriage certificates are issued through the clerk's office.

The New Jersey township government is a representative form of government. The townspeople elect the council members to represent them and to make all of the decisions regarding the township's policies and procedures. The townspeople do not approve the annual budget, the township committee does. However, the townspeople do approve the budget for the board of education.

In New Jersey, the township committee performs all legislative and executive duties necessary to appropriate funds, adopt ordinances, and pass

Early road-building equipment made the job easier, but the methods are primitive compared to modern day equipment. This tractor and scraper appear large until a comparison is made to the size of the operator. (1936, Minnesota Historical Society)

resolutions for the business of the township. These responsibilities require the township committee to serve as the board of health, the planning board, the municipal utilities authority, and the board of adjustment, to name just a few. Members of the committee also serve as the police commissioner, the public works commissioner, and the finance commissioner. New Jersey townships also administer the welfare program, although in the last two years with new legislation many townships have turned that responsibility over to the county government.

Like other states on the east coast, New Jersey is a strong "home rule" state. Municipalities have many authorities and they do not want to give any of that local control to the county or state government, even if it means a duplication of services.

NORTH DAKOTA

There are 1,348 townships in the state of North Dakota, most of which have populations of less than 100. Township boards are comprised of three to five supervisors, a clerk, and a treasurer. The supervisors are elected to a term of three years, while the clerk and treasurer serve a two-year term. The clerk and treasurer can also be a combined position. Held on the third Tuesday in March each year, elections are staggered, allowing for a smooth transition when a new member is elected. Township electors also elect or appoint an assessor.

As the population shift from rural to urban continues, organized townships in North Dakota with small populations may join with up to four other organized townships to form multi-township boards in order to keep local control and prevent the township control from going to the county. There are at least two examples of multi-township boards in North Dakota.

In North Dakota there are 55,000 miles of township roads. Townships have complete responsibility over maintenance, signing, and safety issues. Most of these roads carry the bulk of agricultural products from field to storage and also provide access for the state's fishing, hunting, and other recreational activities. Township budgets are very small, limited to a general levy of 16 mills. Township governments do not have the means to provide municipal services, however they do have control over unincorporated townsites and subdivisions, which may be located within their jurisdictions.

Annexation happens easily in North Dakota, as townships do not have any way to fight an annexation except by public outcry at annexation hearings. Planning and zoning is a serious concern for townships because cities have more authority than townships. Cities with a population of 25,000 or more are allowed to set zoning policies up to four miles outside city limits. As a result, some townships don't have much zoning authority left. Cities with a population of 10,000 are allowed a two-mile limit for zoning policies inside of a township. All other cities are allowed a half-mile zoning limit.

OHIO

The state of Ohio has 1,309 townships in 87 counties. A board of township trustees oversees the day-to-day operations of each township. Three trustees, a clerk, and a treasurer are elected to four-year terms. Elections are held in November of odd-numbered years and terms are staggered to allow for a smooth transition with newly elected officers. The leader of the board of trustees is the president. Township trustees have many duties, some unusual duties include dealing with animals running at large; overseeing the maintenance of ditches, drains, and other surface waters; and viewing property lines between adjacent properties.

Ohio township trustees have the final approval of township budgets. Public hearings are held weeks in advance for residents to voice their opinions, but the final vote is with the board of trustees. The only voice the residents have is when elections are held. Setting the tax levy is defined by state statutes and trustees are allowed only to assess for services the legislature allows. Ohio townships are not allowed to assess an income or earnings tax, only a property tax.

A full range of municipal services is provided by many towns, giving residents police and fire protection, emergency medical protection, parks and recreation, planning and zoning, street lighting, and water and sewer, to name a few. Financing for police, hospitals, and water and sewer service is often done by establishing tax districts for the areas being served by those services.

Road maintenance responsibility is with the townships. The state has more than 40,000 miles of township roads. Townships also manage more than 1,800 township cemeteries across the state.

Currently there are no protections to townships against annexations and townships are threatened with losing land. The Ohio Township Association is working to get statutory help and the association believes it is making some progress.

PENNSYLVANIA

Township government in Pennsylvania is divided into two classes, first-class townships and second-class townships. There is no difference in governing authority between a first-class township and a second-class township. Distinctions are made in population and the type of area being governed. First-class townships are larger and more urban. Second-class townships are found in rural areas and are more agricultural in nature. They also have smaller populations. There are 92 first-class townships and 1,457 second-class townships.

Modern road equipment (such as this grader belonging to Fayal Township in St. Louis County, Minnesota) has become a necessity for many townships. Hiring contractors who supply their own equipment is often more expensive than townships purchasing equipment and hiring a full-time employee. (James Fisher)

A second-class township can become a first-class township if it has a population density of 300 residents per square mile and voters approve the change in a referendum. There are many second-class townships that meet the population density criteria but they have remained second-class townships.

First-class townships are governed by a board of commissioners. There are either five commissioners elected at large or as many as 15 elected by districts. Elections are held in November and each commissioner is elected to a four-year term, with terms of each commissioner staggered. Also elected is a three-member board of auditors and a treasurer. In some counties, townships also elect an assessor. A secretary is a mandatory appointed office and may not be appointed by the board of commissioners. The board of commissioners has final approval of the township's budget. First-class townships provide a full range of municipal services for residents, having separate departments such as police, parks and recreation, finance, water, etc.

Second-class townships have a three- or five-member board of supervisors which governs each township. Supervisors are elected to a term of six years. Also elected is a tax collector and a three-member board of auditors. The secretary is appointed. Second-class townships have a smaller population and therefore a smaller tax base and smaller budget. For this reason they do not provide residents with municipal services. Maintenance of township roads is the only service that most second-class townships provide.

RHODE ISLAND

Rhode Island has only 31 towns and eight cities. There are five counties, but these serve only as judicial districts. Towns must provide residents the same services that counties and cities provide in other states.

Town residents elect a town council of five or seven members, with elections held in November of even-numbered years. Some terms are for two years and some are for four years. Terms are not staggered, so it is possible to have a completely new board elected. A town clerk can be elected for a two-year term, however some towns now appoint a clerk. A town treasurer may also be elected or appointed. Since the town council is considered a part-time council, some towns in recent years have hired or appointed a town manager or a town administrator for daily operations.

Most of the towns still hold annual meetings, allowing the people to approve the town's budget. However, a few towns have passed a charter to give that authority to the town council. Towns are allowed to assess a property tax to pay for the services provided to the townspeople. Larger towns provide a full range of municipal services, while smaller towns can only provide a few services. Many small towns have fire protection through volunteer fire departments. All towns provide road and bridge maintenance.

SOUTH DAKOTA

The state of South Dakota has 942 townships, each holding elections on the first Tuesday in March of every year. Township boards are comprised of three supervisors, one clerk, and one treasurer. Supervisors are elected to a three-year term, however the terms are staggered so only one supervisor is up for election each year. The supervisor who has served the longest is the chairman of the board. The clerk and treasurer each serve a one-year term. There is no limit to the number of terms any township officer may serve.

Townships in South Dakota have many authorities, but the power a township has depends on its composition. If a township has an unincorporated village or town within its borders, the township has some governing authority over that unincorporated town and may pass ordinances dealing with garbage disposal, electricity, street lighting, sidewalk construction and maintenance, water and sewer services, and parks and recreation services. Townships adjacent to a city with a population of more than 50,000 people also have greater governing authority.

Responsibilities of South Dakota's township boards also include township road maintenance. However, for bridges on secondary roads and for culverts with an opening of more than sixteen square feet, the responsibility for maintenance is with the county. The county also has the authority to establish township roads, and may even use township funds along with county highway funds to pay for the construction, graveling, and maintenance of those roads.

Other responsibilities of townships include fire protection, animal control, and the day-to-day operation of governing a township. A township board also prepares and recommends a budget for the people to approve at the annual meeting, held the same day as elections. Some townships work closely with other local governments to provide police and fire protection, and some townships contract with a city, a county, or a private contractor for the maintenance of township roads. These townships are so sparsely populated that it is more cost efficient to contract for those services from other local governments than to own, operate, and maintain their own equipment.

VERMONT

There are 237 towns in Vermont and each performs many of the duties that county and municipal governments provide in other states. The state has 14 counties, but these are for the purpose of judicial districts. Each town is led by a board of selectmen, or more commonly referred to as a selectboard. Residents elect three or five selectmen, depending on whether the town has by charter or by resolution adopted a five-member board. Selectmen serve overlapping terms of between one and three years. Elected with the selectmen are a clerk and treasurer. In many towns, the positions of clerk and treasurer are combined. Some towns have had their residents adopt at the annual meeting a town manager form of government to oversee the daily operations. A few towns have hired an administrator.

Towns have the authority and the responsibility to build and maintain roads and bridges, tax property, control animals, and provide for solid waste disposal. Also, townspeople can decide at the town meeting to allow a town to provide such services as police, fire, and emergency medical protection; water and sewer service; planning and zoning; parks and recreation departments; and libraries.

WISCONSIN

The state of Wisconsin has 1,265 towns, each governed by a town board of three or five members serving a total of 1.5 million residents. The chairperson is elected solely for that position but has no greater power than other board members. Clerks and treasurers are also elected and all officials serve for a term of two years. Elections are held in odd-numbered years on the first Tuesday of April.

Towns are mandated to provide fire protection and many towns are now providing municipal services. Water and sewer systems can be developed provided they are part of a utility district. Towns that provide water and sewer may also have a sanitary district. More than one town may be a part of that district to share costs and a commission oversees this district. Towns also provide road and bridge maintenance for town roads. Twenty-five towns now offer police protection.

Town electors have the authority to levy taxes for the operation of the town. However, a 1985 law allows town electors to delegate the tax levy authority to the town board. A provision in this law also allows the electors to take back the authority if they feel the town board is not handling the responsibility. Currently about 10 percent of Wisconsin town boards decide the tax levy, these being mostly the larger towns in the state.

Towns in Wisconsin are seriously threatened with annexation by cities and villages. State statutes have not provided towns protections here as they have in other states. In 1996, one town with a population of 12,000 had three major annexation plans in process. If all of these had occurred, the town would have decreased to a population of 2,000 and no longer would have been able to function financially. Instead of the three annexations, a major part of the town incorporated into a village, and today that village is annexing the remaining part of the town.

With growing populations, townships face increasing demands for services. Residents expect roads to be cleared of snow within hours after a snowfall, requiring many townships to own equipment. Fish Lake Township in Chisago County, Minnesota has commonly-seen equipment which also provides snow removal when plow and wing attachments are added. (Ray Johnson)

Located in Becker County, Minnesota, the Burlington Township Hall has interesting characteristics seen in many older town halls. (Bill Bliss)

State	Number of Towns or Townships	Smallest Town or Township	Largest Town or Township	Authority to Levy Tax	Road Responsibility	Municipal Services	Elections	Notes of Interest
Connecticut	94 municipalities with town form of government	pop. 610, Union	pop. 139,160, Bridgeport	Yes	Responsibility for all roads	A complete range of services	Charter towns every 4 years, other towns every 2 years, in November	State has no county government; towns provide all services.
Illinois	1,443	pop. 85, Cincinnati Township, Pike County	pop. 191,359, Thornton Township, Cook County	Yes	Road and bridge maintenance of all township roads	A few provide water and/or sewer, police and fire	Every 4 years in April	Townships are mandated to provide general assistance, property assessment, and road and bridge maintenance.
Indiana	1,008	pop. 55, Wabash Township, Gibson County	pop. 178,000, Center Township, Marion County	Total of all levies is set by State Board of Tax Commissioners	None	Poor relief assistance, fire protection	Every 4 years in November	Mandated to provide poor relief assistance, fire protection, and dog licenses.
Iowa	1,588	pop. 57, Morgan Township, Decatur County	not available	Yes, some amounts set by state	None	Fire and emergency medical services	Terms are for 4 years, held in November	Mandated to act as fence viewers and to provide fire protection.
Kansas	1,541	not available	not available	Township board works with county commissioners to set levy	Maintenance of township roads	In Eastern Kansas, townships don't provide many services. In Western Kansas, townships provide many services.	Terms are for 4 years	County government is handling more of the townships' responsibilities.
Maine	440	pop. 28, Centerville, Washington County	pop. 20,808, Sanford, York County	Yes	Responsible for all roads	A complete range of services	Every 1, 2, or 3 years depending on ordinance, usually in the spring	Almost 90 percent of the state's municipalities have the town meeting form of government.
Massachusetts	303	pop. 97, Gosnold, Dukes County	est. pop. 65,000, Framingham, Middlesex County	Yes	Responsible for all roads	A complete range of services	Every 3 years usually in the spring	Allowed to appropriate 5 percent of previous year's levy for a reserve fund.
Michigan	1,242	pop. 16, Point Aux Barques Township, Huron County	pop. 91,735, Clinton Charter Township, Macomb County	Yes	County has road authority	Many services provided, especially in more urban areas.	Presidential years, Primary in August, General Election in November	Mandated for assessment administration, elections and tax collection.
Minnesota	1,793	pop. 11, South Bend Township, Kittson County	pop. 10,852, White Bear Township, Ramsey County	Yes	Road and bridge maintenance of all township roads	A complete range of services	Terms are for 3 years, elections held every year in March	Cities can annex up to 60 acres at a time without argument.

State	Number of Towns or Townships	Smallest Town or Township	Largest Town or Township	Authority to Levy Tax	Road Responsibility	Municipal Services	Elections	Notes of Interest
Missouri	township government in 23 of 91 counties	not available	not available	No, funds come from county	Maintenance of township roads	not available	Terms are for 2 years, elections held in April	Townships serve one purpose and that is to maintain roads.
Nebraska	452	not available	not available	County Board of Commissioners sets budget	Almost all townships own graders and provide road maintenance of township roads	None	Terms are for 4 years	State legislature changed budget authority from township to the county level.
New Hampshire	219	28 pop., Harts Location, Carroll County	pop. 27,378, Salem, Hillsborough County	Yes	Road and bridge maintenance of all roads	A complete range of services	Terms are for 3 years, staggered	Counties exist in this state, but town government holds more governing authority.
New Jersey	247	pop. 62, Walpack Township, Sussex County	pop. 81,550, Dover Township, Ocean County	Yes, township committee approves budget	Responsible for all roads	A complete range of services	Terms are for 4 years	Most major forms of government of all states.
North Dakota	1,348	pop. 3, Sunshine Township, Slope County	estimated pop. 12,000, Grand Forks Township, Grand Forks County	Yes	Road and bridge maintenance of all township roads	Townships are too small	Terms are for 3 years, elections held every year in March	Cities may set zoning policy up to 4 miles within township limits.
Ohio	1,309	several with populations approximately 150	approx. 70,000, Colerain Township, Hamilton County	Yes, for those purposes allowed by law; property tax only	Road and bridge maintenance of all township roads	Many provide a full range of municipal services	Terms are for 4 years and staggered, election held in odd-numbered years in November	Townships manage over 1,800 township cemeteries.
Pennsylvania	1,549	pop. 15, East Forks Township, Potter County	pop. 59,179, Bristol Township, Bucks County	Yes	Road and bridge maintenance of all township roads	First-class townships provide many municipal services	First-class townships have 4 year terms, second-class townships have 6 year terms, elections for both are in November	There are 92 townships of the first class and 1,457 townships of the second class. The position of secretary is appointed by mandate.

State	Number of Towns or Townships	Smallest Town or Township	Largest Town or Township	Authority to Levy Tax	Road Responsibility	Municipal Services	Elections	Notes of Interest
Rhode Island	31	pop. 489, town of New Shoreham	pop. approx. 30,400, town of Middletown	Yes, property tax only	Road and bridge maintenance of all roads	Larger towns provide a full range of municipal services	Some terms are 2 years, some are 4 years with elections held in November of even-numbered years	There are five counties in the state but they serve as judicial districts. Towns perform services commonly associated with county and city governments in other states.
South Dakota	969	pop. 6, Conata Township, Pennington County	pop. 2,137, Split Rock Township, Minnehaha County	Yes	Road and bridge maintenance of township roads, although the counties take care of some	Some provide municipal services, but most do not	Terms are for 3 years, elections held every year in March	Counties can establish new township roads, and may use township funds for construction of such roads.
Vermont	237	pop. 17, town of Victory	pop. 39,000, town of Burlington	Yes	Road and bridge maintenance of all roads	Larger towns provide a full range of municipal services	Terms vary from 1 to 3 years, staggered, elections held in March	Counties exist only as judicial districts so towns provide many services to their residents.
Wisconsin	1,265	pop. 30, town of Cedar Rapids, Rusk County	pop. 22,654, town of Caledonia, Racine County	Yes	Road and bridge maintenance of all township roads	Some towns are beginning to provide basic services	Terms are for 2 years, held in Spring of odd-numbered years	Towns are threatened by annexations as there are no protections allowed by state statutes.

Chapter Four

GRASSROOTS GOVERNMENT

Our government springs from and was made for the people — not the people for the government. To them it owes allegiance, from them it must derive its courage, strength, and wisdom.

—Andrew Johnson
First Annual Message to Congress
December 4, 1865

GRASSROOTS GOVERNMENT DEFINED

When I first became an elected official, the term *grassroots government* was rarely used. I didn't hear it often enough to know exactly what it meant. Or maybe because I didn't know what it meant, I didn't hear it. As time passed, I began to hear it more frequently, with a different definition each time. For example, a speaker talked about the election process and how that is grassroots government at work. A school teacher talked about the beginnings of the United States and how grassroots government was formed. A land developer and a township official discussed a developer's agreement and the grassroots way of dividing land. With all of these differing uses of the phrase, it is easy to understand why so many people get confused about grassroots government. Some people don't like to use the term because it has been misused and has lost its original meaning.

Call it grassroots government and you are saying it is a basic or fundamental government. It is not something old made new again, instead it is something completely new. That is exactly what the government was that Thomas Jefferson and his colleagues created when the Declaration of Independence and the United States Constitution were written. The new government was the foundation for the union of states, for new territories, for governing powers. It was seen in the first township meetings held in small, hand-built township halls as township boundaries were established and citizens elected leaders. You can still see it today, in those same townships at annual and monthly township meetings. Grassroots government is township government, the very foundation of our country's government.

Township officials take pride in the basic form of government they provide to the people. In the Midwest, township boards are generally less frightening than their counterparts, city councils and county boards. Elected township officials are seen as "one of us" and are looking for the most efficient and most inexpensive way of solving a problem with as little red tape as possible. Often the officials go so quietly about their work that you almost forget they are there — until a problem arises which affects you personally.

WHY A TOWNSHIP INSTEAD OF A CITY?

In some states, townships have large populations and they are operated with the same authorities that have been given to cities. They provide many municipal services such as sewer and water, police and fire protection, road maintenance, and parks and recreation, to name just a few. Some New England town governments have larger budgets than cities in their states, and many fund or administer school districts. So the argument can be made that if a township looks and acts like a city, why doesn't it become a city? Some will argue that there are too many townships, that they are too small a unit of government, and they only clog up the system, making it ineffective and a costly duplication of services. Suggestions have even been made to completely abolish small units of government, transferring authority to higher levels of government.

Sitting atop the hierarchy of federal government, it is easy to understand the appearance of many governmental agencies overlapping services. Even working within states, a person can be bounced from one office to another, from state to county to township and back to the county, just trying to get a simple answer to a question. It is enough to make most people throw up their hands in disgust.

But change the perspective by looking at the hierarchy from the bottom. Local government places the emphasis on the townspeople. Townspeople elect their representatives, they attend meetings and make their voices heard, and often they work with the leaders to solve problems affecting the whole community. They are working on a small scale, with relatively low costs, and little overhead. Imagine a city government dealing on a large scale with a population spread over ten or twenty square miles. Costs here would be astronomical for even the basic services. The paperwork alone would lose people and the people's influences would diminish. It is no longer the

As townships became established, many did not own buildings in which to hold meetings so schools and churches were commonly used. Some of these buildings later were purchased by townships and used as town halls and offices. Blowers Township has a population of 330 and is located in Ottertail County, Minnesota. Its town hall was originally a schoolhouse built in 1932. (Bill Bliss) grassroots government it was intended to be. It appears to the people to be a business, and approaching that business for an answer to a problem can be frightening. Suddenly the leaders are no longer "one of us."

What about states with townships already as big as cities, providing many municipal services? Why don't these townships become cities? Usually, if a township is allowed the authority to provide many municipal services, then it also has governing powers similar to a city. The large difference lies in how money is budgeted and who makes the spending decisions. In cities, the mayor or city manager proposes a yearly budget and the council votes on it. In township government, the townspeople determine the budget amount and vote it into place. This small distinction can have a very large impact on the residents of a community. Many annexations of townships by cities have failed for the simple reason that township residents wanted to remain in financial control of the budget.

Some states have given townships greater authority and greater protections from annexation by cities. Michigan is a great example of this with its two types of townships. General Law townships meet the basic needs of a community, following all laws as outlined in the state's constitution. Charter townships are given additional powers for a streamlined administration and greater protection against annexation, and they are allowed to levy larger budgets to meet the needs of the community.

A FIGHT FOR TOWNSHIPS

It is interesting to note that more than 200 years after township government was established, people are still creating townships. Looking for creative ways to keep a community controlled by a local government, unincorporated areas are turning to township government. In the early 1990s, many people in the state of Utah were frustrated with the Salt Lake County board of commissioners and the way land use planning was being handled. The people wanted to have greater control over the planning and zoning of their communities and to protect the original historical boundaries. After months of debate in communities over corporations of cities, the Utah Supreme Court ruled the corporation law was unworkable. The court forced the issue back to the legislature and asked that the law be rewritten. But the debate continued and legislators could not agree on the language to rework the corporation law. As the legislation was drafted, the cities lobbied heavily and several cities petitioning for incorporation were put on hold. Other cities rushed annexation claims to get ahead of any new legislation that would be approved.

In the last few hours of the legislative session, an idea to allow townships to form was presented and a substitute bill was passed. Many legislators admittedly did not even read the bill they voted to approve since everyone was in a hurry to end the session. This final legislation, written and passed in March of 1996, allowed county residents to petition to form townships and gave townships greater powers in avoiding annexations by cities. Townships would continue to receive municipal services from the county, but would be allowed planning and zoning authority. This authority required that annexation and incorporation proposals be approved by the town board, effectively putting an end to annexations. However, the legislation did not give townships taxing authority.

Unincorporated communities were very pleased and immediately had petitions written and proceeded to get the required signatures. The city officials and lobbyists were very irate and sought to have the bill reworked.

The language of the bill required that the vote be a super majority; in other words, a majority of the eligible voters had to approve the formation of a township. If the voter turnout was less than 50 percent of the eligible voters, the township was denied even before counting the votes. The people of unincorporated areas argued that this language did not reflect the intent of the legislature. The cities' lobbyists argued that the language was written just as the legislature meant it to be written. Of course, a case as complicated as this with as much at stake had to find its way into the court system.

Elections were held in 11 areas where the people wanted townships. After the elections were held, the results were sealed and residents waited for a decision from Utah's state supreme court. In 1997, the Utah Supreme Court ruled that the court could not decide what the intent was of the legislators, but the language chosen clearly required a super majority of eligible voters. Knowing that, nine of the townships that had held elections were denied. The results of the vote were in favor of the formation of townships by 80 percent, but the amount of voters were less than the 50 percent required. Only two townships had a super majority and were allowed to form and adopt a town government. But the fight was not over.

During the next year, the cities lobbied the legislature again. Feeling the pressure, the legislators rewrote the entire township bill, taking away all of the governing powers townships were granted only a year before. The residents of unincorporated areas were incensed and great debate was had on legislature policy. Townships are now mute and act as planning advisory boards to county commissioners.

After this legislation failed to allow townships as the people had wanted, many unincorporated communities decided to become incorporated. The Salt Lake County Board saw this as a potential loss of the tax base and knew taxes would have to be raised. At present, there is a strong push by county commissioners for areas to incorporate all at once. Commissioners feel it would be better to raise taxes one time to account for the lost tax base.

Frustration is still the emotion for many of the residents who had petitioned for a town form of government. These people wanted local government to control the annexations, not county commissioners and city councils. They wanted a government for the people, by the people. They wanted local control over their communities. Instead, they have to speak loudly at city and county council meetings and in city and county elections.

VOLUNTEERS

A government *for* the people, *by* the people requires the work *of* the people. As mentioned earlier, some townships are as large as big cities and provide many municipal services. They have the means to levy taxes for those services, since townships with greater populations can afford to provide more than less populated townships. But no matter how big or small, township government is rooted in the efforts of the people in the township. Look behind the scenes and you will find many volunteers doing some of the work.

Using volunteers from the community is one of the ways in which townships can keep costs down. All across the country townships rely on volunteers, often unnoticed, quiet in their work, receiving no glory or compensation other than a reward of serving their communities. Many planning commissions and parks and recreation boards are made up of unpaid, dedicated individuals. Some townships have even involved the local Boy Scouts or Girl Scouts to build picnic tables or plant flowers in a township park or maintain the grounds of a township cemetery. Other townships have involved the entire community in spring cleanup days, beautifying the township while saving countless tax dollars. Many senior citizens play active roles in their communities helping with general assistance needs, providing transportation for other seniors, and serving in senior community centers.

Ask any township board member how many hours he or she devotes "free of charge" in any given month and the number will surprise you. They are rewarded by serving the people, keeping governmental controls local. Ask those same officials why they devote countless hours to their communities and you will get a variety of answers. But in the end, the desire for a township government that serves the people is the motivating factor.

PUBLIC SERVANTS

Township officials are indeed elected to their positions, receiving modest payment for their service. In some states, the authority that township officials have is limited, which narrows the duties they perform. In other states, township officials wear many hats, performing numerous duties that affect

Across the country, town halls come in many shapes and sizes. Crow Wing Lake Township in Hubbard County, Minnesota has a population of 210. Its town hall has a handicapped-access ramp to its 16' by 20' building. There is also a ramp which leads from the left side of the building to the outdoor restroom. (Bill Bliss)

most members of the communities. No matter the type of government, the scope of duties, or the number of hats worn, all elected officials are public servants. Elected by their constituents, they fulfill the duties of the office to which they were elected.

Issuing licenses for pets, maintaining cemetery records, acting as fence viewers, and destroying noxious weeds all appear on the surface to be some of the less-involving duties of a township official. But even these duties can become complicated in a hurry. Some examples: A township resident has a permit to have deer on his property. A neighbor's dog likes to agitate the deer, which are contained in a fenced area. The dog continues to irritate the deer to the point that the deer feel threatened and hurt themselves trying to escape the fenced area. Asked by the owner of the deer to impound the dog, the official has to inform a family that its pet is being taken away and may possibly be destroyed; an emotional issue that township officials like to avoid.

Township officials also deal with privacy issues. An example of this is in the administration of cemetery records. Fifty years ago, a woman gave birth to a child and the father was not identified on the birth certificate. Tragically, the child became ill and died. Many years later, a relative is researching genealogy records and wants the information on the child and the parents. The law clearly states that some of the information is private, so the township official does not give out that information. Frustrated, the genealogy researcher is left without answers.

Frustration is also a common element when an official is asked to be a fence viewer. In some states, this means working with a landowner to keep a fence in good order. It doesn't seem important to some of us, but it can mean quite a lot to a farmer who wants to protect livestock. In some states, acting as a fence viewer is a matter of relocating property lines. It involves dealing with adjacent landowners who have become argumentative with each other to the point of calling an official to establish the boundary between two properties. Relying on township survey records, landowner records, and marker stakes put in the ground many years prior, a township official must try to calm landowners and find an answer to the problem or find a professional surveyor approved by both neighbors. This is a difficult task to perform with angry neighbors.

A final example of issues becoming complicated lies within the duties of destroying noxious weeds. Once each year I attend a meeting in which I learn about the noxious weeds in our area, how to identify them, and to which office I should report them. When I tell people about this part of my job, they often smile and question the difficulty in watching out for noxious weeds. But consider the farmer who has a crop in his field in which he has invested

Townships in Iowa are mandated by state law to manage cemeteries. In other states, it is common for township governments to oversee the management of local cemeteries. Established in 1800, Belltown Cemetery is located in White Hall Township, Greene County, Illinois. Even though it has "town" in the name, this cemetery is not a township cemetery. (Bill Bliss) countless hours of time and thousands of dollars. Another landowner nearby on a hobby farm likes the look of a noxious weed called musk thistle. The hobby farmer doesn't know this is a noxious weed, and likes the weed's cute little purple flowers that look like covered buttons. The hobby farmer lets it thrive along the frontage of his property, and in a few months, the weed is killing the farmer's crop. The farmer wants damages from the hobby farmer for the lost crop and approaches the township board to demand the weed be destroyed. A simple issue of destroying weeds is now complicated and may have cost a farmer thousands of dollars.

As public servants, often our duties are numerous and complicated. In many states township officials administrate welfare programs, school districts, and hospital districts in addition to managing the daily operations of running a township. The hats we wear are many and colorful, and some aspects of our jobs are more comfortable to us than others. In dealing with those who have elected us, we are reminded that we are chosen to serve them, to provide them with a service. It is not easy to put a smile on our faces when called at three-o'clock in the morning and being asked when snowplows will be going out. Yet, we are the ones who know that information and we are to serve the public and provide them with the answers they need. In the wee hours of the morning we may not be very cordial, and may even wonder why we continue to be an elected official. But at the end of the day, when the roads are cleared of snow and the township is abuzz with talk of surviving another blizzard, we can take pride in knowing we served our community and met the needs of the people who chose us.

Which leads one to wonder, just what motivates a township official to run for re-election term after term, sometimes serving for twenty, even thirty years? I have been asking that question for some time now, every time hoping to find someone with a "one-liner" answer that sums it all up. Well, I'm still searching for that cute answer.

Instead I have gotten lengthy answers, each person having a different myriad of reasons. Even when I have asked myself that same question, I struggle to answer in less than 100 words. Some people find a great reward in giving back to their communities, while others like being involved and making a difference in policies and procedures. There are some who first were elected at an early age, who stayed with it for thirty years because it was a comfortable fit. "Who else is going to do the job?" that official may ask. There is also a certain camaraderie among township officials and that appeals to some. Undoubtedly for some, the feeling of power motivates them to continue, although voters realize this quickly and take that to the voting booth. Voters have the greatest power in deciding who will stay in office. Often it is a sign of approval to an official who is allowed to serve for twenty years or more.

Township officials wear many hats, meaning they have many responsibilities and are involved in many interests. Because of this, officials often have to be careful with conflicts of interest. Once a person becomes involved in his or her community, that person can become involved in more than one way. A township official may also be a member of the local chamber of commerce organization or some other community service organization. Many volunteer firefighters are also elected township officials. Township officials may also work for a local business. At times our professional or personal interests may cross lines with the day-to-day business of running the township. It is then that we need to step back and carefully examine the issues. If a township official has the potential to personally or financially gain from a township decision, the official must abstain from the decision-making process. If someone perceives a conflict of interest in an elected official's vote, then that elected official has a duty to abstain from such a decision. Conflicts of interest are oftentimes very controversial and delicate issues, and they have been known to change the outcome of many township elections.

COMMUNITY INVOLVEMENT

One does not have to become an elected official to become involved in township government. Large townships have numerous boards and commissions comprised of local residents.

Larger townships, which offer a variety of municipal services, require many different individuals to sit on planning and zoning boards, boards of adjustment, parks and recreation boards, sewer and water commissions, fire district boards, police commissions, boards of health and family services, environmental commissions, public utilities commissions, and in some states, boards of education. Many townships now publish a newsletter put together by residents willing to devote their time. Any resident with an interest in a certain topic can find a committee or commission of which to become a member. Some of these positions are paid and some are volunteer.

Smaller townships don't have the numerous commissions and boards for residents to chose from, however there are still many areas in which to get involved. I know of several retired people who work about 10 hours a week for townships, getting simple chores done and keeping costs down. These people act as janitors for township halls and community centers, or hang road signs and install mailbox posts for new homes. Some are retired professionals serving as certified building inspectors. Having these individuals perform such tasks keeps the townships from having to hire a full-time employee. Many townships depend on local residents to provide services to the people that would otherwise be cost prohibitive to perform on a local level and would have to be done at a county level. Often the pay is minimal, but great rewards are given to those who serve, in terms of pride and of giving something back to their community.

ELECTIONS

The surest way to get involved in your community is to run for an elected office. Being in the midst of a political campaign is quite an education, no matter how small the number of votes. Residents of your community will call you and ask your opinions on different topics, whether you support a certain policy or if you intend to make changes once in office. You may be asked many personal questions that are inappropriate for a township election, but an elector learns much about you by your response or by how you refuse to answer the question. You suddenly find yourself in the mainstream of politics and you learn much about your community and its residents, and even more about yourself.

Campaigns and elections are as varied across the country as is township government. Qualifications for a township official are usually as basic as being 18 years old and a resident. No matter what size population a township may have, circumstances within the community may bring many candidates who will vie for a single position. Issues may be hotly contested. If a controversial issue is being contested in the campaign, you might see a handmade flyer mixed in with your weekly shopper newspaper and a few signs on township roads. If there is public outcry against an incumbent, you will likely hear a buzz among the talk in coffee shops and see even more flyers and more signs.

However, if the business of the township is perceived by the townspeople as being run efficiently, then there will likely be no controversies. In these circumstances, oftentimes an incumbent will run unopposed and won't even send out flyers or put up lawn signs. Local residents may be reminded of the vote, but turnout will likely be small. If no one is feeling personally affected by the way the township is managing its business, there will be no change of officials in the election. Township government gives the vote to the people and quite often the people speak loudly of dissatisfaction by voting officials out of office.

The process of an election begins many weeks before a resident goes to the voting booth. Every state has different election laws, but the basics are the same. Candidates have a certain time period to file and pay a filing fee. This puts the candidate on the ballot. If a candidate changes his or her mind, then there is a certain time allowed to withdraw and take the name off of the ballot. Next, a certain period of time must pass before the election is held. Many townships in recent years have used this time to hold debates with the candidates, or informational meetings for townspeople to get to

Gust Jacobson and Tom Danielson — 96 years old — casting their ballot at Carrollton Township General Election Nov. 3-1942

Two elderly gentlemen were photographed as they voted in the Carrollton Township (Fillmore County, Minnesota) general election, Nov. 3, 1942. Today election judges and voters are dressed more casually, but the business at hand is still taken as seriously as it was when this photo was taken. (Minnesota Historical Society) know the candidate and his or her views on township policies. Campaign literature is used at this time and as an election gets closer, more campaign signs will appear.

Some people don't follow the traditional method and instead opt for a write-in campaign. There are many reasons for this, but the most common reason is because the write-in candidate didn't decide to run for the elected position until the last minute. This can be a very difficult process and quite a challenge to win.

At this writing, I have been involved in five elections. Four elections were for the position of township supervisor, and of those four, two were write-in campaigns. In my first election, I was asked to run two weeks before the election by members of my township. After deciding I would, there was much work to be done. I sent out a flyer and people volunteered to make signs for me. Numerous phone calls were made informing people of my decision to run and answering questions again and again. I was very surprised when I won by a vote of 102 to 61.

Three years later I was unsure of whether I could handle the responsibilities of a township supervisor because I was expecting my third child. When I didn't file for the election within the allotted time, my phone rang constantly. The townspeople liked the job I was doing and urged me to continue. Prior to that I had been doing my job quietly, with no one ever telling me they disliked or even liked my performance. I had no idea so many people appreciated the job I was doing. Again, I launched a write-in campaign and won a contest among four candidates with almost twice the number of votes of my nearest competitor.

The next two elections I filed in the appropriate time period, paid the filing fee, sent out flyers, and made yard signs. Phone calls were made and I even knocked on doors answering questions and encouraging people to get out and vote. I was fortunate in that the townspeople believed I was still doing a good job of representing them.

The fifth election I have been involved in was the most recent. In the state of Minnesota, we have an organization called the Minnesota Association of Townships. There are 13 directors who comprise the board, all elected township officials. Each director represents a district comprised of about 150 townships in the state.

When the filing period for the position of director was open for my district in June of 1999, I did not file. About a week before the election was held, I was strongly urged by township officials from my county to accept a nomination at the district meeting and be included in the election. In a sense, it would be a write-in election. I did not send out any flyers, I did not put up any signs. Local township officials made a few phone calls. When I won the election, I was the most surprised person in the room.

Many times I have said township government is a quiet government. Officials go about their work behind the scenes, quietly getting the job done. As representatives for the townspeople, we always get complaints and rarely hear words of praise for a job done well. It is an honor to win an election, because it is the most direct way townspeople can speak to you about your work performance. It is an even greater honor to be elected by your peers to serve as a director for your state's township association.

An election is quite an education. Win or lose, you learn much about your community, your townspeople, and yourself. You experience firsthand the democratic process. If successful in your bid for public office, you often discover sitting on the other side of the table is more difficult than many leaders make it appear.

ANNUAL MEETINGS

Perhaps the greatest community involvement in township government occurs at a township's annual meeting. It is this meeting that determines the true identity of township government, because the townspeople have the power to make major decisions affecting policies, personnel, and financial matters of the township.

Townships in some states hold annual meetings at the same time as elections, usually in the spring. State laws require certain hours for voting, with the annual meeting following after the voting booths are closed. Other states hold elections in November as part of general elections, then hold annual meetings in January or early spring. No matter when the annual meeting is held, the purpose is the same: to allow registered voters of the town to act as a governing body, deciding such issues as road construction and repair, tax rates, and the township's annual budget. It is a time when the voters can debate local issues and inform the elected officers as to their wishes. No other form of government allows the taxpayers so much governing power, and for this reason township government is often referred to as the purest form of democracy, hence grassroots government.

TAX SYSTEM

The quickest way to begin a long conversation is to ask a person what he or she pays in property tax. People everywhere have an opinion that they pay too much and get too little for their tax dollars. Planning experts even offer proof of that when they tell elected officials that a new house will not pay enough tax to support the "living" services required. Township government is unique because it allows the taxpayers the right to set the budget, and in doing so they

Many townships still use paper ballots for every election. In recent presidential elections, many election judges served a total of almost 24 hours between judging and counting. (Ray Johnson) choose what their tax burden will be. If taxpayers want more services, they must be willing to approve a bigger tax burden. Still, when that tax bill arrives in the mail, telephone calls to local officials are guaranteed.

With population increases in recent years, many townships have turned to hiring administrators or managers to help oversee the financial operation of government. Some townships have even elected to take the final approval of the budget away from the taxpayers and have given that authority to the elected officials, much like a city. New Jersey is one such state, as the township committee approves the budget. Public hearings are held to discuss the budget, but the final vote lies with the township officials, not the townspeople.

Tax systems can be complicated and confusing. Elected officials struggle in trying to explain a particular system and to justify a tax bill. This is when an administrator or manager would be a good addition to a township's personnel. I have found it helps to simplify a property tax bill by breaking down the tax bill into categories. How much of your tax bill goes to your county? How much to your school district? How much of the total truly goes to your township? Quite often people are surprised to learn that only a small percentage of the total bill goes toward their local government. In my county, most townships receive about ten percent of a taxpayer's property tax. When I look at that small amount, I realize I'm getting quite a bit for my money. But it also makes many wonder what the county is offering taxpayers when it receives almost half of each property tax bill.

In states where county government plays a small role and townships offer most of the municipal services, the tax burden will be shifted and the majority of a property owner's tax bill will be going to the local government. In this instance, the taxpayer feels the cost is justified because so many services are being provided on the local level, such as sewer and water, police and fire, and parks and recreation, to name a few.

ROAD SYSTEM

Ask any township official what causes the most phone complaints, and nine times out of ten the answer will be roads. Townships by their nature give the people a voice, and road complaints are heard loud and often, at all hours of day or night.

Our township has a snow plowing policy that states snow accumulations of three inches or less will not be plowed. I have received phone calls after a two-inch snowfall asking me why the plows are not out. I have also received complaints after a four-inch snowfall when the plows went out and taxpayers thought it unnecessary. You can't please everyone.

Roads are the biggest concern for most townships and road budgets reflect that. In Missouri, townships exist only for one purpose: to maintain roads.

Missouri townships have road budgets which come from the county but the townships have local control of the roads. Many times the county government in Missouri has tried to eliminate townships, but the voters won't allow it. Taxpayers want control over the condition of their roads to remain at the local level.

There are a few states with town government in which the county maintains local roads. In Iowa, townships have small populations and little tax base, so township budgets are very small. It is more cost-effective for county governments to maintain roads. In Michigan and Indiana, the counties maintain roads and receive money from the townships to do the work. For the most part, township officials are happy to be free of the responsibility. However, there is a growing concern among taxpayers that local government could do a better and more efficient job at a lower cost. This will be an area to watch in the coming years, especially since new legislation is expected to be introduced in Michigan in 2000 to allow townships to maintain their own roads.

LEGISLATIVE IMPACT

Of the 20 states that have the township form of government, ten have a state organization like the one mentioned previously, the Minnesota Association of Townships. These organizations are very active in their states, especially in pursuing a legislative impact to better their communities. The names of these organizations are:

> Connecticut Council of Small Towns
> Township Officials of Illinois
> Indiana Township Association
> Michigan Townships Association
> Minnesota Association of Townships
> North Dakota Association of Township Officers
> Ohio Township Association
> Pennsylvania State Association of Township Supervisors
> South Dakota Association of Towns and Townships
> Wisconsin Towns Association

Each of these state associations has a specific mission, but similarities abound from state to state in the goals these associations want to achieve. Each association serves to provide a unified voice for township government and its officers. These associations conduct research and educational programs for efficient, effective, and economical township governmental services. They influence legislation, policy, and regulations by representing townships before the state legislature, executive office, and other state agencies. They also aim to promote a public understanding of the heritage and the future of township government.

Having a direct impact on state legislation is important work for these state township associations. Township governments are small units of government and therefore cannot afford to, nor do they have the means to, lobby state legislators to protect themselves. State associations can speak loudly in a unified voice and often they do. There are several examples throughout this book of how legislation has been changed to protect or maintain township government. More progressive townships have faced issues and overcome obstacles and through state township associations have helped other townships face those same issues with less difficulty.

In addition to state associations, townships are also served by the National Association of Towns and Townships (NATaT). The purpose of NATaT is to strengthen the effectiveness of town and township government, by educating lawmakers and public policy officials about how small town governments operate and by advocating policies on their behalf in Washington, D.C. NATaT holds an annual meeting of all townships, which serves as an educational and legislative conference, helping township officials be more effective representatives. The conference week in Washington, D.C. also provides a time for township officials to lobby Congress on issues important to the townships. The greatest reward for me in attending this conference is meeting other township officials, sharing common problems and some solutions that have been tried. It is a great opportunity for me to learn new ideas and to learn from another township's mistakes. It is easy as an elected official to get too narrow a focus and become preoccupied with our own township's issues. Having a chance to talk with other officials from across the country helps get us out of that narrow focus and into a broader frame of mind, opening up educational possibilities.

Chapter Five

TOWNSHIPS IN TODAY'S WORLD

The legitimate object of government, is to do for a community of people, whatever they need to have done, but can not do, at all, or can not, so well do, for themselves — in their separate, and individual capacities. In all that the people can individually do as well for themselves, government ought not to interfere.

—Abraham Lincoln
July 1, 1854

Working With Other Local Governments

All across the country, communities are dealing with urban sprawl and sustainable growth. People from metro areas are moving to more rural areas, and those rural areas are struggling to stay rural. Local leaders are looking to plan for the future, while allowing new subdivisions to be built today. And with higher populations, residents are demanding more services. Often, the tax being levied to the properties cannot provide the services being demanded. How can a township give the residents what they are asking for but without taxing the residents out of the area?

More often townships are looking to neighboring communities to create service districts or joint powers agreements to provide the services that are being demanded. There are many success stories of towns and townships joining together to form fire districts to offer that protection at an affordable cost. Many townships contract for services with cities or counties for police protection. Some townships have been very creative in solving local problems, others have had long fights that left residents with bitter feelings about local government.

The successes are stories we all like to hear about or tell one another. Those accomplishments not only get a job done or a problem solved, but they also give residents a good experience with local government. Some residents may even decide to get more involved as the result of a project that achieved a goal for the community.

However, there will always be the other stories, the ones in which problems are not solved and are possibly made bigger; the ones in which people can't speak to one another or won't let their children play with other children because of a difference of opinion among the parents. These stories don't make any local officials proud. In fact, they are the events that make us all wonder why we stay involved in local government. Sometimes these situations cost residents money, sometimes they cause changes in township boards at the next election.

There are lessons to be learned in both the successful stories and the not-so-successful stories. We need to communicate with one another to find solutions at the lowest cost, in the most efficient manner. We need to learn to live together, even if that means local authorities from neighboring communities must tolerate each other. There will always be a problem that needs a solution or a question that cries out for an answer. Sharing ideas and working with other governments will often make the crisis easier to solve. If not, then we need to learn from the experience so we won't have to face that particular problem again.

Following are some examples of local governments working together, trying to solve common problems. A problem may appear on the surface to be simple, such as building a community park, but underneath lies the issues of costs, maintenance, and liabilities. Other problems may be insurmountable, such as local officials struggling to turn back flood waters while their own homes are being destroyed. There is an old adage that says even the most difficult of tasks can be accomplished by taking one step at a time.

Joint Powers Agreements

The most common tool used by a township when cooperating with other local governments comes in the form of a joint powers agreement. This legal agreement allows different governments to jointly hold power for the purpose of providing a service to their residents. There are several ways such an agreement can be used to provide fire and emergency medical service, animal control, planning and zoning, road maintenance, and many other services. Several townships may join together in this agreement, or a township and a city, or any combination of township, city, and county government.

Providing a service in the most cost effective manner is the principle behind joint powers agreements. Many governments would be financially pressed to provide a service without such an agreement, and there would be an unnecessary duplication of services. By using a joint powers agreement, two or more governments can share costs and equipment, and yet provide a quality service to citizens.

As is always the case with two parties working together, differences of opinion may occur. Joint powers agreements, when carefully written, will address common concerns and problems to avoid disagreements. Negotiations for renewal of such agreements can be very frustrating. It is not impossible to keep personal feelings out of such negotiations, but it is often difficult. Elected officials have a responsibility to provide a service in the most cost effective way possible. With joint powers agreements they also have a duty to negotiate an agreement to work together for the common good. There are times when the arguments become so great that the leaders lose sight of the primary purpose of the agreement.

FIRE PROTECTION

For some states, such as Iowa, providing fire protection is mandated by state law. Townships must provide this service to residents no matter the cost. For other states, fire protection is not mandated, but the residents have voted to increase their taxes to have fire protection locally based. Many larger townships which provide numerous municipal services have large budgets and therefore large fire departments. However, most townships have small budgets, relying on small, volunteer fire departments to meet the needs of the township.

In many parts of the country one can find fire departments with the word *township* in their names, such as Wayne Township Fire Department in Indiana. This department is one of the largest volunteer fire departments in the country, having about 400 firefighters and averaging about 30 calls a day. However, it is *not* a township fire department. The Wayne Township Fire Department is a private corporation, as are many other fire departments that have *township* in their names. Some of these fire departments cover a large area which may include more than one city and parts of several townships. These fire departments may have large budgets, contracting for services with several local governments.

A true township fire department, one owned and financed only by a township, is rare. Townships have struggled with budgets, trying to make ends meet and yet provide a quality service for residents. With state and federal regulations changing constantly, it is extremely difficult for these small departments to manage on limited funds. Not only do the firefighters need proper protective clothing and properly maintained equipment, they also need expensive training to deal with modern society's needs. We no longer ask our firefighters to come to a fire scene with a simple water truck. Now we want

A fire department may have the word township in its name, but it may not truly be a township-owned fire department. Many fire departments are the result of joint powers agreements between townships, cities, and towns. Some are even private corporations, contracting for services within their districts. (Monica Dwyer Abress)

them to respond in a set amount of time and enter burning buildings to save parts of those buildings. We now ask them to be prepared to deal with a medical emergency or a hazardous chemical spill. More and more fire calls are dealing with traffic accidents on major thoroughfares. We are asking firefighters to be on-call for more responsibilities, such as finding lost children or watching for damaging storms. Townships are financially unable to afford the type of service residents demand today.

Cities and townships are working to form joint powers agreements as a way of providing effective fire protection in as cost effective a manner as possible. Fire districts are being created, allowing several local governments to share costs and equipment. Mutual aid agreements are made among several fire departments to help one another during major fires or rescues. A willingness to cooperate is the thread binding these agreements.

Yet, in many parts of the country, the binding thread is getting frayed. Cities and townships are finding it difficult to work together, accusing each other of raising budgets without justifying costs. Fire chiefs are finding themselves defending their expenses and the costs of replacing necessary equipment.

In the state of Iowa, experts have been studying fire departments since 1997. What the experts have found concerns them greatly. The Fire Service Institute, a division of the Iowa State University Extension Service, sent out surveys to all of the state's 99 counties, getting 100 percent response. The institute asked for information on fire protection and how local governments finance this service. George Oster, program manager of research and development for the Fire Service Institute, shared some startling statistics. Eighty percent of Iowa's fire departments serve a population district of 5,000 or fewer. Of these, one-third are operating on budgets of $20,000 or less. Nine percent of the state's fire departments are operating on a budget of $5,000 or less. Twenty percent of the state's townships cannot afford to provide any fire protection, even though it is mandated by state law.

According to Oster, these budgets are low for several reasons. Fire departments are not adequately communicating their needs to the local governments, and therefore are not getting the necessary training and equipment to deal with today's types of emergencies and the demands of residents for more services. Only twenty-five percent of all firefighters in the state of Iowa are certified Firefighter I.

Cities are not funding fire protection properly because of a state mandated property tax freeze. Cities are allowed $8.10 per $1,000 for *all* of the services a city must provide. City councils must pick and choose which service needs the funds.

Townships have a maximum limit allowed by the state to levy for fire department protection, but many townships are taxing only half of that amount. In fact, some townships are levying more for cemetery upkeep than for fire protection. Another interesting fact is that townships are taking in more money for fire protection than is being spent. The state does not require that townships be audited like cities, so there are no clear answers on where the money is going. This causes distrust from cities which have joint powers agreements with townships.

The Fire Service Institute recently presented the study to the legislature with a list of suggestions for change. The institute believes cities, townships, and fire departments must each play a role in improving current conditions. Simply raising tax levies is not the solution. Increased levy amounts for townships may actually lead to a decrease in amounts cities are willing to give for fire protection. In order for city councils to trust township boards, township governments may need to become financially accountable to the state in the form of an annual audit similar to that of the cities. Cities and townships need to cooperate by creating written agreements that include a formula for cost sharing. Fire departments must work at coordinating and scheduling regular training sessions, and work to communicate needs to local governments. Even the state needs to get involved in providing financial assistance for training, and in developing a statewide education and training system easily available to all parts of the state. Iowa's experts are watching the state's legislature to discover what changes legislation will bring in 2000.

The findings of the fire institute's report are issues we all need to consider. In order to continue to provide an affordable quality service of fire protection, local governments will need to remain partners in joint powers agreements, working together for the common good. If residents will continue to demand many services, and if local governments will continue to place added responsibilities on firefighters, then we must all be prepared to pay the price, no matter the cost. The price may seem high when the tax bill arrives in the mail, but when it is your house or business on fire, you will pay anything to have quality fire protection nearby.

RURAL SEWER SYSTEMS

Known as the land of 10,000 lakes, Minnesota has many homes and cabins sitting on small lots bordering its lakes and rivers. The majority of these buildings were built many years ago, before sewer regulations were passed. Because of this, many have noncompliant sewer systems, systems that do not meet state regulations. Adding to the problem, many lake and river lots are notoriously odd shaped and small in size, a result of developing more lots fronting the water. These small lots do not have the state-regulated minimum required distance between the drinking water well and the wastewater system, creating potential contamination of the drinking water. Minnesota is not alone in this problem.

Environmental concerns have become common discussions in recent years, and people have looked for ways to deal with these noncompliant sewer systems. There are many solutions to upgrading a noncompliant system, provided there is space on the lot to do so. With lake and river lots, the space is not always there.

In the early 1990s, Wabedo Township in Cass County, Minnesota found a unique solution to upgrading noncompliant sewer systems on lake lots. The township board became aware of a state statute that allowed a service to be provided to a defined portion of the township. The township board then contacted property owners to make them aware of the statute. After meeting with the township board, a group of eight homeowners petitioned the township to create a subordinate service district to provide a sewer system for their homes. A subordinate service district is a defined area within the township in which one or more governmental services are provided specifically for that area and financed from the properties involved. With the district in place, a sewer system could then be developed and necessary financing arranged.

The system design called for each property to have its own septic tank and be connected to a main sewer line that carried effluent to a treatment tank and drainfield. The disposal area was located on soils suitable for drainfields far enough away from the lake to meet all state standards. Benefiting property owners arranged a repayment plan with the township for their share of the project.

Maintenance of the system needed to be addressed and the township found a creative solution with the local rural electrical company. The utility agreed to manage the system, charging an annual fee to the property owners which is added to their electric bills and collected for the township by the electrical company. The fee is minimal; the electrical company's plan is not for profit. The fee covers the cost of a monthly inspection of the drainfield and system, maintenance of the grounds for the drainfield and system, and pumping of the system at two-year intervals. The electrical company, through a subsidiary security company, provides "round-the-clock" monitoring in case the sewer system has a problem. Arrangements have been made with electricians, sewer contractors, and sewer pumpers to be available at a predetermined fee in case a problem arises. Once a year the electrical company meets with the township board to determine a maintenance budget for the next year and to address any concerns.

Difficult to see in this photo are words cut into the bottom of this entrance gate announcing the Pike Bay Town Hall. Pike Bay Township is one of the larger ones in Cass County, Minnesota with a population of 1,490. (Bill Bliss)

Wabedo Township has two of these wastewater systems in place, each successful in operation and management. Across the state of Minnesota, other townships are also looking at this model with various stages of implementation in place. This is a unique solution that has been proven affordable and effective, as well as a great environmental improvement.

FLOOD PLAIN AGREEMENTS

A small town in Indiana, Elnora lies just east of the White River. A levee was built in the late 1920s to help hold off flood waters for about a mile and a half of the river's frontage. At the time the levee was built, a levee board was established to oversee the building of the levee and its maintenance and repair. The levee board quit functioning in the 1960s. There was a period of about 25 years with no major floods and people forgot about the levee's importance.

Of course, nature raised its fury again and the river rose to above flood levels in 1991 and 1993. The town's residents were fortunate, as the levee held for both major floods and only a small part of the town was evacuated. If the levee had failed in either of the floods, 75 percent of the town would have been ruined. With the community threatened by flood waters twice in three years, residents were concerned about the old levee and its ability to continue to offer protection.

The Army Corps of Engineers conducted a study that said the levee was in very poor condition. In its recommendation to the town, the corps stated it would not be economically feasible to repair the levee. Elnora, with a population of 700, did not know how it would pay for a new levee. The town hired a contractor to give an estimate on necessary repairs to the levee, just to keep it in operating condition. The cost estimate was $120,000.

By the urging of the town's leader, community activism was brought to life as residents made phone calls and began a letter writing campaign to state assembly members. Asking for the $120,000 for repairs, residents reminded the legislators of the recent floods and promises made at the time to help with repairs. Legislators agreed to give the amount for repairs and turned the money over to the Department of Natural Resources (DNR). The DNR then conducted a study of the levee and declared the money given toward the project would not cover the necessary repairs.

Elnora elected officials and DNR representatives lobbied the state assembly for more funding. In the end, state and federal funds were awarded and the levee will be completely rehabilitated at a cost of more than $1 million. The project came to life in designs on paper in 1997, and work will begin in early summer of 2,000.

ANNEXATION BY CITIES

Townships across the United States are efficient forms of government, providing services for the township and the townspeople at the lowest cost possible. There are times, however, when the townspeople want services that the township cannot afford. Sometimes townships are able to negotiate for services with another local government, but at other times the costs of the services are exorbitant. Many times townspeople want the specific service and are willing to request their portion of the township be annexed to a neighboring government to get that service. The most common example of this is a city annexing a part of a township to provide city water and sewer service. The townspeople want the service of city water and sewer, but the township cannot afford to install a township water supply and water lines, nor provide wastewater treatment. Another example involves a new housing or commercial development requesting water and sewer service. A developer may ask that the land involved be annexed to a neighboring city as a way of hooking up to the city's services. Annexations such as these occur often and generally without much fight. As a result, townships are literally losing ground all across the nation. Cities are growing outside of their boundaries and looking to the townships to provide the land.

Some cities are in a different predicament. Populations change within cities which causes federal and state fundings to change. Cities then look to neighboring townships to annex land as a way of increasing populations to receive those federal and state funds, and as a way to increase a tax base. Townships have been favorable to this as residents can see added benefits and services that will be provided to them as a result of the annexations. There are times, however, when a township is providing so well for its residents that annexation by a city will not provide added services. In fact, annexation may be a burden to the township residents and increase property taxes or cause a drain on a vibrant community.

In northeastern Minnesota, an annexation fight has occurred between a city and a township several times over the last 20 years. The fight began in 1973 when the city of Eveleth approached Fayal Township to inquire about the two entities consolidating. Fayal did not want this, so the city then looked at annexing a portion of the township. The discussion grew and soon many parts of Fayal Township were being looked at for annexation by two other adjacent cities as well as Eveleth. After many months of discussion, a vote was held in September 1976 in the cities of Eveleth and Gilbert. Each city was looking to annex a portion of Fayal Township. The annexation vote passed in Gilbert but failed in Eveleth, and no land was annexed at that time.

Following the vote, Fayal Township passed a resolution to petition the state municipal board for incorporation as a city. Shortly after, the city of Eveleth reconsidered the portion of Fayal Township that it originally wanted to annex and filed a new annexation request with the state municipal board. In December of 1977, Fayal was denied incorporation. At the same time Fayal was turned down, Eveleth held a special election on the new annexation and the vote passed. But Fayal Township filed a complaint with the District Court citing numerous election violations. Six months later the fighting between area residents continued and property owners in a platted area in the city of Gilbert petitioned to be annexed to Fayal Township. That annexation was allowed to take place in June 1978. It took until March of 1979 before Eveleth heard its new annexation request was denied.

The battle was not over; it was dormant. Area residents were still dissatisfied with the services being provided by the city to the township. In 1984, Fayal Township formed a Police and Fire Commission to look at ways to provide better service to its community. More than a year later, the commission reported that Fayal Township was not getting adequate fire protection from the city of Eveleth, recommending the township organize a volunteer fire department. The Fayal township board acted on the commission's recommendation and the Fayal Fire Department began providing service in September 1986.

In 1991, the city of Eveleth and Fayal Township formed a consolidation committee to research the most effective way of providing services to their residents. Again, many months passed with lengthy discussions and in October 1992 the committee reached a conclusion that the idea of consolidation was inappropriate at that time. However, further study was encouraged. Fayal accepted the committee's recommendation while Eveleth did not, and Eveleth submitted a request to the state for the consolidation. Fayal saw this as a move toward a hostile takeover.

At the same time that the consolidation committee's report came in, the right to vote on annexation very quietly slipped away from state statutes through a tax omnibus bill in the Minnesota state legislature. Townships were caught unaware that the right to vote was no longer allowed. Fayal Township residents no longer had the basic right to decide their township's future, so fears of a hostile takeover worsened. The argument for consolidation went on and turned into another discussion of annexation in December 1997.

The annexation battle grew more complicated in early 1998, when Fayal Township decided to clean up four of its ten lakes and put in a sewer system to the homes and summer cabins on those lakes. Eveleth already used one of the four lakes for its water supply, so Fayal approached Eveleth about the possibility of hooking into that water system and also hooking into the city's sewer system. The Fayal Township board asked the Eveleth city council to give an estimate on the purchase of water for some of the townships 2,000 residents. Eveleth quoted the township a price of $5.40 per thousand gallons for bulk water to be distributed to the residents along the four lakes involved.

After reviewing the quote, the Fayal Township board felt Eveleth wasn't giving a fair price. So Fayal looked to another neighboring city, Gilbert, for another quote on water supply. Gilbert looked at the opportunity as a way of earning a profit and, in turn, a way of repairing and improving its aging water system. Gilbert quoted Fayal Township a price of $1.95 per thousand gallons for bulk water. This was quite a difference in cost from the quote given by Eveleth and immediately questions were raised about the integrity of the Eveleth city council. The fight was on again.

Tempers were flaring and people took sides. Letters to the editor appeared weekly in local papers, accusing many people of wrongdoings. Residents of Fayal Township shopped in Eveleth and had children attending Eveleth public schools. The mayor of Eveleth at the time was quoted as saying Fayal residents used Eveleth's library and other public buildings, and they drove on Eveleth's streets, but they didn't pay any taxes for those services, so they shouldn't be allowed to use those services.

Eveleth continued its pursuit of annexation, arguing for expansion of boundaries for redevelopment and residential growth, an increase in population to over 5,000 for additional state financial aid, coordination of emergency services, and coordination of planning for long-term services such as sewer, water, and planning and zoning. Fayal sent its own letter to the state municipal board voicing objection to the annexation. Fayal officials believed the township was self-sufficient and accused the city of Eveleth of a hostile takeover for additional state aid (which amounted to $200,000) for municipal roads because of an increase in population as a result of the annexation. Fayal officials stated that annexation to Eveleth would require additional police protection at a cost of $65,000 to give the township the same protection the city had. If annexation occurred, the city would have another 57 miles of road to maintain for a total of over 87 road miles. With the state aid for road funding, the city would have an additional $2,300 for each road mile. Fayal officials believed that amount would not provide for necessary normal road maintenance, and they believed they were doing an effective and efficient job of providing all services to township residents.

Other townships in the county sent letters in support of Fayal Township to state legislators. Eventually a bill was allowed into consideration by the Minnesota House of Representatives that would return the right to vote on annexation. At present, the state legislature is reviewing the bill. However, the state municipal board in February 1999 denied Eveleth's latest request for annexation. Fayal Township entered an agreement with the city of Gilbert to install sewer service around four lakes and construction has begun. The project should be completed in the fall of 2000. With the request denied for annexation by the state municipal board, the hostile takeover issue has quieted down. But some of the area's residents still have bitter feelings. Some residents feel the fight has not died but is dormant.

Bitter feelings are a common element in annexation struggles. Townspeople and city residents fight such major issues as property rights versus community interest, controlled growth versus urban sprawl, us versus them. Even after an annexation dispute reaches a conclusion, bitter feelings can remain. Yet, townspeople and city residents must find a way to continue to live in proximity and share the use of businesses and schools.

In Coventry Township, near Akron, Ohio, annexations had occurred several times over many years. Townspeople grew bitter at the progressive sprawl and the urban problems that came with it. They were quickly overwhelmed by the city's power and felt their community was threatened.

The city, on the other hand, was looking for solutions to problems rooted in growth and prosperity that followed World War II, for at that time the city had prospered and many buildings and homes were built. Now, those same buildings and homes were badly in need of repair and updating. The city's infrastructure (roads, curbs, gutters, sidewalks, etc.) was also outdated and the tax base was not growing as it should to support the redevelopment the city needed so desperately. In order to redevelop, the city needed a bigger tax base and looked to neighboring townships to annex land. In the early 1980s, the city began a very aggressive annexation policy and took many acres of land. The breaking point occurred in 1985 when Akron annexed the prestigious Firestone Country Club.

Township residents were furious and bitter feelings were prevalent in all. The only people benefiting were the attorneys, as they argued numerous annexation disputes and just as many changes in the laws and ordinances. The city of Akron wanted land from neighboring townships with present and future businesses and the income tax associated with that business to pay for the redevelopment of the older part of the city. The townships wanted independence and the protection of their property tax base.

In the late 1980s, two elected officials came together to find a way for local governments to cooperate for the better of the entire community. The mayor of Akron, Don Plusquellic, and Coventry Township Trustee Val Sawhill, were tired of the years of bitter feelings and two governments colliding instead of working productively side-by-side. By this time, Coventry

Township was only one third its original size from its beginnings more than 200 years before.

It took over six years of negotiations, meetings, and intensive lobbying, but an historic agreement was reached and passed into legislation for the state of Ohio. This agreement took the name of Joint Economic Development Districts (JEDDs) and was passed into law in 1994, affecting only Summit County where Coventry Township is located. In 1995, JEDD legislation was extended statewide.

The agreement between Akron and Coventry Township called for:

- The return of 146 acres of land to the township that had been annexed by the city over the last 200 years.

- A truce of no annexations until the year 2090, with an option for two 50-year extensions which would extend the agreement to 2190.

- The township to keep the property taxes generated within the JEDD district.

- The city to continue to provide water and sewer services to the JEDD district, vital to future business expansion.

- The city to receive a corporate and individual income tax revenue from the JEDD district.

- The city to give to the school district a 12 percent net allocation of the income tax revenue.

In the state of Ohio, townships are not allowed to collect income taxes. So under this agreement, the township was able to keep the land for the property tax base and the city was given an income tax generated within the district. The city needed that income tax to help fund the redevelopment of the older parts of the city. It also felt there would be a loss to the school district by not including the students residing in the JEDD district, as they would not attend the city's schools. For that reason, a 12 percent net allocation of the income tax funds was earmarked for the city's school district. Water and sewer services would continue to be provided to the area, a necessity for business to expand. During the first six years of the agreement, 50 percent of the income tax revenue generated would go toward extending sewer and water lines into the JEDD area.

Only 12 percent of Coventry Township is in the JEDD area. People who work in the JEDD district pay a 2 percent increase in their income tax which goes to Akron. For city water users within the JEDD area, there is a 10 percent surcharge. For extended service areas, there is a 22 percent surcharge. However, water and sewer rates are still the lowest charged outside the city's limits.

Initially, businesses were opposed to the JEDD agreement. They had built or moved to the townships as a way of avoiding paying an income tax and they did not want to start paying that now. The agreement was contested and argued all the way to the Ohio Supreme Court. In March 1999, the legality of the JEDD was upheld.

The rules to establish a JEDD are clearly defined in the Ohio state statutes, but briefly an agreement can be reached by following these steps:

- Develop a JEDD contract describing responsibilities of the city and township.

- Hold public hearings on the contract.

- City council and town board legislatively adopt the contract.

- File the approved contract with the county and county legislative approval is given.

- Submit the contract to a township electoral vote for approval.

- Form a JEDD board consisting of three township trustees, Mayor, two elected city officials appointed by the mayor, with all board actions requiring five of six votes for approval.

As a result of the JEDD agreement between Coventry Township and the city of Akron, other agreements have been made and future agreements are planned between the city and three other townships as elected officials see many improvements to their communities. Those townships now feel new development is controlled and placed in specific areas for growth, and townships benefit from an improved property tax base. New development at the city's border is environmentally safe, connected to the city's sewer and water system. The city now has an income tax to redevelop the oldest part of the city, providing the potential for growth and financial rewards to the city. Even the city's schools have an improved financial position.

But the most important benefit of the JEDD agreement can be found in the absence of bitter debates among local governments. No longer are annexation struggles argued in the homes, on the streets, in businesses. Communication is working well between the city and the townships, and local governments are working together on mutual terms, for the better of the entire community. Akron Mayor Don Plusquellic and Coventry Township Trustee Val Sawhill have each been given awards for establishing the JEDD agreement.

LOCAL GOVERNMENT IN THE SCHOOLS

History or civics teachers have in their curriculum a lesson plan on state government. Occasionally a discussion will take place regarding city and county government. Rarely does the discussion include the township form of government, except to mention it in a discussion of early American history. One of the reasons I decided to write this book was to help get the word out to students across the country about township government and how it is alive and operating quietly in thousands of communities.

The reason it is so important that students learn about township government is because they are the leaders of tomorrow. There has been a nationwide decline in public participation in local government in recent years, and the reasons attributed to this are many. However, one such reason is a lack of education about local governments, about what local government does, and how it works.

In September of 1995, a program was started in the town of Ludlow, Massachusetts called "A Local Government Partnership." Local officials were struggling to get new people involved in local government, so these officials decided a place to start would be to teach students about local government and how they could participate. A meeting was held with all local government officials in the school district asking for volunteers to teach about their duties to high school students. Officials from all departments and all types of government were asked to be involved. The list included police officers, tax assessors and collectors, members of finance committees, boards of selectmen, town clerks and treasurers, members of boards of health, school board members, town planners, zoning administrators, even state senators and representatives.

The idea behind the curriculum was that each board or department would have an official teach students about the duties of a particular job. The school course would run a full semester, and officials would come in for one or two days, teaching high school seniors in a local government class. The lesson plan called for each senior to learn about the duties of selectmen, how a finance committee prepares a budget, how assessors figure market values and assess taxes, how town planners affect the growth in a town, and on and on. For every official who volunteered, the students learned about that person's job and how it related to local government. In the process, the students learned quite a few differences among township, city, county, state, and federal governments. In addition to the classroom lessons, the students were required to attend two town meetings.

Local officials were invited to a meeting to get this program started. Dennis Rindone was the coordinator and at the time was the western regional manager for Massachusetts's Division of Local Services and a selectman in the town of Erving, Franklin County. Rindone said the number of local officials and government employees who attended the meeting was better than expected, and everyone who signed on to the program did an excellent job. The people who became the teachers were very helpful, took the responsibility seriously, and were committed to the program, according to Rindone.

In June of 1999, this program was in ten local high schools, involving five communities and more than 500 students. As a result, many students were appointed to planning commissions, parks and recreation boards, and other subcommittees of the local governments. At one annual town meeting, 60 high school seniors were in attendance to see town government at work.

These students were made aware of local governments and were taught how they can become involved and make a difference in their communities. The program was created out of a wish to involve more young people, and its success can be measured by the number of students who took the lessons outside the classroom to apply in their towns. No one can know how many leaders of tomorrow were encouraged by this program.

Chapter Six

TOWNSHIPS OF THE FUTURE

"...this nation, under God, shall have a new birth of freedom — and that government of the people, by the people, for the people, shall not perish from the earth."

−Abraham Lincoln, Gettysburg Address,
November 19, 1863

LAND USE PLANNING

A major discussion is taking place all across our country regarding the way we divide and use our land. In many states there is a push to create green corridors, areas of open spaces that form bridges of undeveloped and preserved land. In the discussion, environmentalists are loudly trying to protect the earth's natural resources. At the same time, people are demanding larger lots for their houses with improved services and shopping areas closer to their homes. How do we create a balance? How do we meet the perceived needs of the people *and* protect the earth for future generations? How do we decide which services we need to have in our communities? Do we need to have all those we want? The challenge is to balance our needs while protecting the things that contribute to our rural quality of life.

One important item to remember in this discussion is survey lines. More than 200 years ago survey lines were drawn to create townships. Some of those lines have been moved and therefore the boundaries of cities have changed. With that change of a line on a map can come a change in school districts, property tax and assessment amounts, legislative or judicial districts, even a change in fire, police, and emergency medical districts. We may think moving a line will create more services for an area, but we may not always look at all of the consequences of that change.

Land use planning is a difficult task. It requires us to predict what our community will be like in twenty, even fifty, years. Some of us are better at predicting than others. We may have lived in an area for most of our lives and from that experience can predict what the future holds and how well we can handle it, given our current resources. Still, some of us may be newcomers and want to protect the main attractions that brought us in the first place, not allowing any more progressive changes to occur. Are we willing as residents and as township officials to say "no" to developers? Do we have the confidence to say "no"?

ZONING

With land use planning comes zoning, the process which establishes rules and regulations for an area. For those states that have county governments, county zoning administrators are well-known individuals in every county. Their administrations dictate building codes and zoning ordinances, and issue new building permits, wastewater systems permits, and many other permits.

For most townships, the county planning and zoning commission has final approval on all zoning concerns within the township. A township may have its own planning and zoning commission that makes recommendations to the county's planning and zoning commission, but the final decision is with the county's commission. In recent years, this decision-making process with control at the county level has caused great concern for many communities.

With the spread of populations into rural areas across the country, county zoning offices are being overwhelmed with new building permits and numerous housing developments. Understaffed and overworked are the common justifications for permits being issued in error or for oversights when inspections are completed. Township officials have grown frustrated with permits being issued that they didn't approve. Residents and township officials have questioned the ability of county officials to know and understand all areas of a county. Township officials believe they can better plan for their local areas, and therefore should have the final decision in zoning matters.

In recent years, many townships have adopted zoning ordinances where allowed by law. Usually the laws in these states require a township's ordinances to be as restrictive or more restrictive than a county's ordinances. This restriction has been a welcome change for many townships. Officials in townships that have passed zoning ordinances feel more in control of the future of their communities. They are satisfied with the decisions being made on a local level, even though this process has increased their responsibilities. Across the country, more and more electors are being asked to approve such changes in zoning administrations as word spreads that this process can be successful in gaining local control.

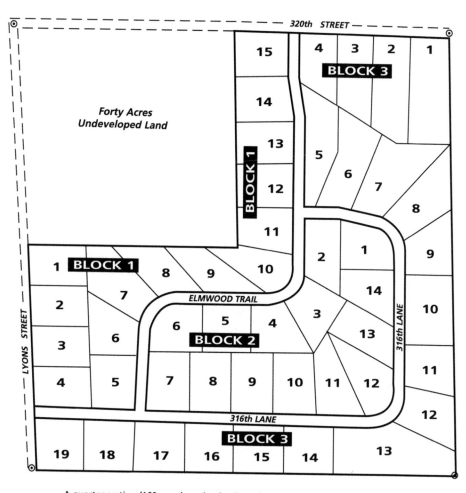

A quarter section (160 acres) can be developed numerous ways. This subdivision plat puts 48 homes on 120 acres of land, while the remaining 40 acres stay undeveloped and in agricultural use.

It is an understatement to say county zoning administrators are not happy with this change. They have concerns that townships do not have the trained personnel to perform all of the necessary inspections on buildings and sewer systems, as well as many other inspections. County administrators know firsthand how quickly an office can be overwhelmed with work, and they fear townships will not be able to handle the demand. In fact, some zoning administrators believe more harm than good will come from allowing townships to have local zoning control. Uncontrolled growth and urban sprawl could result.

RURAL SPRAWL

Here's a phrase that has entered the English language in recent years: urban sprawl. It means that new development is spreading out from a city's limits. We've all watched this happen in our urban communities. New houses are built just outside of a city's limits, and soon there are convenience stores and gas stations offering services close to these new homes. Next, small shopping malls (or strip malls) are built in these new areas, offering even more shopping convenience close to the new homes.

The same type of growth is happening in our rural areas; an appropriate name for this is rural sprawl. Many townships that were once major farming communities are seeing low-density residential developments being built on agricultural land. The demand for homes on two- to five-acre lots has driven up land prices, which in turn has enticed some farmers to sell their land. With less land to farm, it is more difficult for remaining farmers to find land to rent for their operations. As a result, we end up with large amounts of land split into fragments that are not suitable for agricultural uses or as habitats for wildlife. Perhaps state legislatures should be persuaded to provide more incentives to farmers to hold on to their land, or to place it in conservation easements or land trusts.

Blending new development with agricultural land uses creates many problems. New rural dwellers are not used to the noise and odors of farming operations and tensions begin to build. Also, experts have frequently told us that the costs of providing services to a new home are greater than the tax revenue generated by the new home. For the farmers who have lived in a rural area for many years, their taxes begin to rise as townships try to continue to provide services. It doesn't take long for arguments to begin between the new rural dwellers, the farmers, and township officials. A wise farmer once told me, "Government let all these houses come in and ruin the township. Government can make changes to deal with it." So how do we deal with it? How do we satisfy the needs of people wanting to live in a rural setting, but at the same time keep the setting rural? Perhaps the answers to those questions are found in still another question. How far is government willing to go in setting policy to deal with rural sprawl?

PRESERVING RURAL CHARACTER

Many people are attracted to the open spaces of rural areas, the "simple" lifestyle seen in smaller communities, the "character" of an area. Once new development comes in, bringing homes and business, the rural character begins to change. Roads built to handle farming operations are now challenged to deal with hundreds of cars each day. New residents unfamiliar with on-site septic system maintenance create, by negligence, problems with sewage disposal and water quality. Increases in population require increases in police and fire protection. Schools struggle to maintain small class sizes, in existing buildings, while student populations swell. And local officials are held accountable by residents who demand the township's rural character be preserved. How do we preserve rural character? Is it already too late?

In order to preserve rural character, we must first know how it is defined for our community. This definition will vary from community to community, and will differ among the residents in a community. Long-time rural residents may see the rural character of a community in terms of farm operations, limited services, and homes on parcels no smaller than 40 acres. Newcomers may romanticize a community of quaint homes with picket fences on two-acre lots and small family-owned businesses and services conveniently nearby.

With such differing viewpoints, how do we define rural character for our community? Do we look at the natural environment and traditional rural lifestyles, then try to preserve them? Or do we forge ahead into an unknown future, trying to please newcomers and old-timers alike? Do we look only within the boundaries of our communities? Perhaps we need to look at why people are attracted to our rural communities. Why are people leaving the metropolitan areas? Why are people so willing to commute for hours each day to jobs in areas where they don't want to live?

We also must ask ourselves, who will be responsible for defining the rural character in our community? Do we rely on our elected leaders to make this decision based on their knowledge of the community? Many monthly city and township business meetings have issues being discussed and decided that will impact the area's rural character. Often those monthly meetings are poorly attended, and the voices of only a few are being heard. So in reality, an area's rural character is being defined by the opinions of only a few residents and the elected officials. How can we justify our complaints in the future when we were not in attendance at the time important decisions were made?

TOWNSHIP SURVIVAL

Many states have felt pressure for some time to eliminate township governments. In largely populated areas, the push to do this has been very successful. Cities of all sizes have taken over lands of neighboring townships; some annexations are done quietly, others with a lot of noise and a big fight. In rural areas, the argument has been debated that a township form of government is more cost effective and a city-type government would be cost prohibitive.

To the elected township official, and to the township resident, township survival should be a necessity. No other form of government gives the people so loud a voice in decisions that affect their pocketbooks. No other form of government allows the taxpayers to set policies and evaluate the business of their community once each year. Township government has been called the truest form of democracy still in existence. How can we let that disappear?

If we are not careful, township government will disappear. In many states annexations occur regularly and townships have little or no protection against them. Townships are literally being erased from county maps. Townships are struggling in many areas of the country to deal with rural sprawl and sustainable growth issues. Often townships are restricted by state laws and therefore they cannot adequately change to meet the needs of the townspeople. If state legislatures do not give townships authority to pass ordinances to meet the demands of the people and to control zoning on a local level, more and more petitions will be presented asking cities to annex township lands.

For those states that have given townships some protections against annexation, we need to better educate township officials and residents alike. Many townships have the authority to provide a service to residents by creating a service district and an agreement with a neighboring city. Yet oftentimes, the residents or the officials are unaware that this is an option. Residents petition for annexation with the belief that annexation is the only way a service can be provided. To be as efficient as they are, townships have learned to be creative when it comes to meeting the needs of the residents. By educating officials and residents better than we have been, we will help end unnecessary annexations.

As township officials, we must learn to open our minds to new ways of thinking. We need to step out of the box of limited thinking, and look to other communities for alternatives and new solutions. Many states offer regular training seminars for township officials on countless subjects affecting township governments. These seminars should be a top priority and be attended by all elected officials. Not only can we learn from the topics being presented, but also by mingling with officials from other communities, sharing problems and solutions being implemented.

Township officials also need to work harder at convincing other local government officials that townships serve a purpose in today's world. With critical examinations across the country of the need to reduce taxes and downsize governments, our job won't be easy. One thing in our favor, though, is the basic principle of township government, giving the people the right to self-government.

In the end, how we handle the issues in our townships will determine our survival. Keeping road authority in the community is of prime concern for many township residents. Control over tax dollars has kept many communities from abandoning the township form of government. Allowing townspeople to voice their opinions and know they are heard is crucial to township government's survival. Quietly going about its work, township government is efficient and effective. The future will challenge township officials to find new solutions to common problems. We will be called on to work more with other local governments to continue to offer services at affordable costs. Involving more youth in our commissions and committees will ease us into tomorrow's leaders, providing our grandchildren with a quality of life we can feel good about.

Experts often ask people across the country about their lifestyles, their measure of happiness, their quality of life. From these studies, an argument can be made equating township government and a high quality of life. The next time you see a newspaper article or hear a news report on the radio or television about the top 10 states to raise your children, pay attention to the names of the states. People reporting a greater happiness and a better quality of life are often from states that have the township form of government. There are 20 states that have township government, and a listing of the top ten most livable states will include a majority of those. Is it a coincidence? Or is it possible that township government provides people with a way of life that makes them feel good about their communities?

Township government has been in place for more than 200 years. It exists for the people, by the people. The future holds many difficult challenges and they will be overcome one at a time, for the people, by the people. For it to be a democracy *for you*, you must be involved. Step up to the table and voice your opinion, volunteer your time, sit on a commission or committee, get involved, make a difference.

STATE TOWNSHIP ASSOCIATIONS

CONNECTICUT
Bart Russell, Executive Director
Connecticut Council of Small Towns
1245 Farmington Avenue, #101
West Hartford, CT 06107
860-521-4774
Fax 860-561-1040

ILLINOIS
Bryan Smith, Executive Director
Township Officials of Illinois
408 South Fifth Street
Springfield, IL 62701
217-744-2212
Fax 217-744-7419

INDIANA
Indiana Township Association
5664 Catio Drive, #120
Indianapolis, IN 46226
317-562-4927
Fax 317-562-4932

MICHIGAN
John LaRose, Executive Director
Michigan Townships Association
512 Westhire
Lansing, MI 48917
517-321-6467
Fax 517-321-8908

MINNESOTA
David Fricke, Executive Director
Minnesota Association of Townships
Box 267
St. Michael, MN 55376
612-497-2330
Fax 612-497-3361

NORTH DAKOTA
Byran Hoime
North Dakota Association of Township Officers
6750 92nd Avenue NE
Endmore, ND 58330
701-644-2720

OHIO
Michael Cochran, Executive Director
Ohio Township Association
5969 E. Livingston Avenue, Suite 110
Columbus, OH 43232
614-863-0045
Fax 614-863-9751

PENNSYLVANIA
B. Kenneth Gredier, Executive Director
Pennsylvania State Association of Township Supervisors
3001 Gettysburg Road
Camp Hill, PA 17011
717-763-0930
Fax 717-763-9732

SOUTH DAKOTA
Gail Brock
South Dakota Association of Towns and Townships
P.O. Box 903
Huron, SD 57350
605-353-1439

WISCONSIN
Richard Stadelman, Executive Director
Wisconsin Towns Association
W7686 State Highway 29
Shawano, WI 54166
715-526-3157
Fax 715-524-3917

NATIONAL ASSOCIATION
National Association of Towns and Townships (NATaT)
Tom Halicki, Executive Director
444 N. Capitol Street NW, Suite 208
Washington, DC   20001-1202
202-624-3550
Fax 202-624-3554

GLOSSARY

Annexation: the act of annexing (taking) territory.

Annual meeting: occurring once each year, this meeting allows registered voters of a township to act as a governing body, deciding such issues as road construction and repair, tax rates, and the township's annual budget.

Charter township: a township that has adopted a specific set of ordinances or laws, making it distinct from other townships. Often a charter township is allowed more authority than a noncharter township.

Geographical township: a territory in surveys of U.S. public land measuring 6 miles by 6 miles, containing 36 sections or 36 square miles.

Grassroots government: a basic or fundamental government.

Green corridors: areas of open spaces that form bridges of undeveloped land and preserved land.

Home Rule: a state statute that allows a township to enact a set of laws, providing those laws do not go against the state's constitution. Home rule is found in only a few states. A state which has home rule, allows townships that adopt it greater authority to pass ordinances governing all aspects of the community.

Joint powers agreement: a legal agreement allowing different government entities to jointly hold power for the purpose of providing a service to their residents. Used most often to provide fire and rescue service, police protection, and road maintenance.

Land use planning: predicting future needs and planning for use of land for agricultural, residential, industrial, recreational, or other purposes.

Mill rate: a formula used in some states to determine tax assessed value of property. One mill equals one-tenth of a cent, or $.001. Some people use the term *tax rate* instead of *mill rate*.

Public servant: a government elected official or employee.

Rural character: the distinguishing features of a rural area.

Subordinate service district: a defined area within a township in which one or more governmental services are provided specifically for that area and financed from the properties involved.

Super majority: a majority decision of all eligible voters. For example, if 100 people are eligible voters, then at least 51 must be present and vote in favor of a decision in order for it to pass. If less than 51 people vote, then the decision is not passed regardless of the vote totals.

Sustainable growth: planning for controlled development being careful to not permanently change, deplete, or damage an area or its resources.

Tax levy: to impose a tax to receive funds to provide a service or services.

Township: a unit of local government found in 20 states.

Urban sprawl: the uncontrolled spread of urban development into neighboring areas. In recent years, this has affected rural areas as well, creating pockets of development in undeveloped areas.

Zoning: the process which establishes rules and regulations for an area.

INDEX